I am a fan! This book is brilliantly and intelligently written. The rich descriptive adjectives, figurative and literal language, sensory elements that this book offers, rocks my literary world and inspires me to have bigger faith in what is around us and what is to come. It is an anointed book and I received some unexplained healing by simply reading the book.

While reading, I was reminded of authors like John Flanagan, CS Lewis, and JRR Tolkien. They are all masters at writing descriptive language about imaginative places. The difference is, Blue writes about real miracles. It is evident with her writing talents why God chose to gift her with these visions and then commanded her to "write them down". You won't want to miss the passages that lay between the covers of this book.

Have you wondered about the majestic, beautiful, and awesomeness that awaits us in heaven? Maybe you are interested in mystical angels that interact with us and dance around us daily? Are you seeking information about the power and victory the name Jesus has over the enemy? If you answered yes to any of these questions, this is your book!

It opens with a sweet and kind note from the author. In parts I & II, you will read about awe striking moments when the veil is thin. Part III takes a different turn toward spiritual and Biblical teachings. Some readers might find this part a lull, but it has pearls of wisdom. I read this book with a pen and highlighter. Stay with it because the book finishes strong in part IV with more visions and finishes with a sweet update from Blue.

It is evident that Blue is an experienced Biblically based believer. She references the Bible frequently and she states that she has read the entire Bible multiple times. She is also an avid reader herself and likes to be challenged by what she reads. This is shown when she shares that she has read all 30,000 words that Teresa of Avila wrote (not an easy task to read 500 year old language).

This book is a bridge between Roman Catholics and Protestants. With my spiritual history, I feel 100% at home in between the pages of this book. I think this book will not only bring healing to individuals, but also to the Christian Church as a whole, to the remnant. It will be a balm to the rift of 1517. I am now a fan and will read every book this author writes!!

~ Angela Francis
English Teacher & Former Catholic Youth Minister

As I sat down to read "My Demon My Jesus" I felt as if Blue and I were sitting on her back porch looking out over the fields when she began to tell me her story. I reflected on my childhood as she shared hers. I felt her pain, her angst, her love of Jesus, her rebellion, and her return. I saw her visions through her eyes. When she shared how to be "saved" I saw with new eyes what it really meant…. My soul was made alive. I was a new creation. I was encouraged to continue getting to know my Lord and follow where the Holy Spirit leads. What my life holds may not be through tongues or visions but Jesus has a plan for my life. I am excited to see what transpires.

Once you start reading you will not want to put it down. See what God wants to do with your life.

~ **Lawrence Reynolds**
Amazon Review

"Wow!" …in a good way, was my reaction after the first few pages and then at the end of the book it was another "Wow!"

My goodness I found her story to not only be an easy read but very engaging and inspirational. Some of it hit me right in the gut, but that's real life… I think it must have taken a lot of courage for Blue to have written her story but I'm so glad she did. I believe many readers will be inspired, have hope and find the strength and courage to get through the Darkness. Loved it! I've already recommended it to several.

~ **J. Hall**
Amazon Review

This book has inspired me to seek Jesus in a whole new light. Wonderful book about a journey to discovering our Heavenly Father. You won't want to put this book down.

~ **Joan Tripp**
Amazon Review

Reading "My Demon My Jesus" was a reminder that I am a simple human, and like everyone else, possessed of a roughly three pound brain. There is only so much horsepower available and many things (like "eternity", "infinity", "omniscience", and "omnipotence") are beyond my ability to comprehend. God is way, way above my pay grade. God is here, but it isn't my job to define or even understand who or what God is.

So I approach stories like Blue's with an open mind and an open heart. What do I know? Oppressive demons? Malignant possession? Sure. It's not my story, after all. I don't have to understand.

That said, in telling her story she touches upon some fundamental truths we, as individuals, as a culture, and as a society, have largely lost sight of. She writes:

"We think we are defined by our thoughts and beliefs. But really this prattle rattling around in our brains is not much more significant than our fickle emotions."

Let that sink in. I suspect I knew this in my bones as a child and forgot it after years of navel gazing and education, of feeding my self-image lies and creating a wall between myself and God. This is a very important thing and at the very heart of "My Demon, My Jesus".

We hear cliches--"Let go, Let God", for example—but it is difficult to get out of our own way sometimes. Blue patiently explains, through telling her own story, how she got out of the way and accepted her place in creation. That resonates.

Another unspoken theme is another simple truism: we get better and better at whatever we practice. If we practice being prayerful and present we become more present and prayerful. If we practice worry and attempting to control things outside of our control, we become worrisome and frustrated, pinched and mean and spiritually hobbled.

This is a valuable book. I'll read it again and again.

~ **Mark Trumble**
Amazon Review

MY DEMON
MY JESUS

Delivered from Demonic Oppression & Suicidal Depression; Brought Back from Death into Victorious Life, Divine Joy & Visions

by Blue Tapp

2022

Unless otherwise indicated, all Scripture quotations in this volume are from the New International Version Bible.

First Printing 2022
ISBN: 9798836653767
Imprint: Independently published

send inquiries to:
Blue Tapp
Hermit's Way Homestead
89 Doc Miller Rd.
Blue Eye, Missouri 65611

bluetapp.com
facebook/blue.tapp
twitter.com/BlueTapp
instagram.com/bluetapp/
youtube.com/channel/UCo36NW3KqOuUDpl2g362AuA
truthsocial.com/@BlueTapp
rumble.com/c/c-1204664

Cover design by: Blue Tapp

TABLE OF CONTENTS

Psalm 4:3-4

The LORD hears when I call to Him… Meditate in your heart upon your bed, and be still.

Psalm 18:16-19 (NIV)

He reached down from on high and took hold of me; He drew me out of deep waters.

He rescued me from my powerful enemy, from my foes, who were too strong for me.

He brought me out into a spacious place; He rescued me because He delighted in me.

MESSAGE FROM THE AUTHOR

I believe God has arranged for this book to end up in front of your eyes for a reason. And I've prayed for you. I pray that God blesses you. I pray that the words in this book will help you find something you are looking for. I pray that you will be physically well, emotionally healed, and spiritually whole. I pray that ultimately you will learn to rest in the glorious love of Jesus Christ, and reach the victory and joy that are available to us through Him during this physical life. I'm praying for these things for you right now as I write these words and I will continue to pray for this. May God bless you, my friend.

Blue Tapp

1997. DEATH.

I am determined not to fail this time.

I buy several boxes of sleeping pills and tediously cut each pill out of the blister packs with scissors until twenty little white pills lie in a grim heap on my kitchen table.

I don't even sit and stare at them for a while first. There is no hesitation. No doubts. I want to end all of this. I grab them up in one big handful and gulp them all down with a glass of lukewarm water.

I have finally done the thing that will kill me. I feel no fear. There is only peace and relief. I have finally done it. All the years of tortuous planning, the failed attempts, the agonizing ever-present despair… this painful existence will all be over soon. My demon will no longer have a host. I lay down on my couch and drift off to haunted sleep and wait to die…

I wake hours later in the middle of the night. The walls and ceiling twist down and curve around me in curious angles. I watch them, fascinated by their strange oscillations.

I slowly become aware of voices urging me to "Wake up! Wake up!" I look around the room. Who is calling me?

Four immense beings stand in the middle of my living room staring down at me. Their heads almost touch the old cracked twelve foot ceiling. They are transparent, shimmering white, luminous, and beautiful with strong smooth masculine bodies and faces. Their long white robes gently sway back and forth at their feet. They have no wings but I know they are angels. The walls are faintly visible behind their translucent bodies. They remain completely still except for their soft flowing robes. Their stoic faces and eyes watch me in the dark room. I am mesmerized. I somehow know they are here to help me.

They insist, "Wake up! Wake up!" Their mouths do not move. They speak to me through some telepathic way directly into my mind. Their voices are whispered but strong, urgent.

For a long time I watch them, trying to understand. I am drugged and heavy from the pills. My thoughts are sluggish. Finally I grasp their words. I am too confused to act. I say outloud to them, "I don't know what to do…"

Their commands become more specific… "Call for help. Call 911…"

At last I understand. Maybe I don't really want to die after all.

I drag my body off of the couch and crawl across the floor to my phone. The angels keep urging, "Call for help! Call 911!" Their voices push me forward. They cut through the drugged fog and give me strength. "Call for help! Call 911!" and so I push the buttons on my old landline phone.

The operator picks up. "Hello what is your emergency?" I say something like "I tried to kill myself and I don't want to die anymore." Then my mind collapses into emptiness…

My next memory is of floating near the ceiling in a brightly lit corridor. People walk back and forth below me as I drift through the hallways. I am not in control. I only observe what is happening. Slowly I move through a crazy maze of bright hallways. Masses of people rush to and fro beneath me. No one notices me hovering above them.

I approach a doorway, descend to the ground and stand on the tile floor. Inside the doorway is a large fluorescent lit room and people seated in chairs. I recognize later that I am in a hospital, looking into a waiting room. Right now I have no idea where I am or what is happening to me. I feel no fear, only calm curiosity.

I walk into the room toward a woman sitting in a chair holding a baby. She is young with long dark hair. Her baby is tiny, a few weeks old. I walk toward her and she looks up at me. I am shocked that she sees me. I stop directly in front of her and feel myself smiling at her. She looks back up at me, surprised. I reach down and she lets me take her baby and hold it in my arms. I gaze into the baby's sweet face and bend forward to kiss his cheek. The tiny child sleeps in my arms. I smile at the woman and gently hand the baby back to her. She stares at me, her forehead creased in confusion.

BOOM!

The room shakes. The woman, her baby, the floor and chairs, instantly disappear. I am hurled backwards as if a giant invisible fist has struck my chest.

In a single moment I rush back through the same maze of hallways I had slowly traversed earlier. People flash below me faster and faster until they become blurry smears of color.

BOOM!

I stop abruptly in a large bright room, hovering for a few seconds by the ceiling. Below me lies my own physical body on a table. Medics lean over my body.

There is a third explosion and I blast back into my body. A sharp pain slices through my face and head and my back arches up from the table. A long gutteral moan reverberates through the antiseptic air. It is my own voice.

Then everything is black.

DECEMBER 2019. JESUS.

The sky is a tempest. Black, purple and blood red clouds eddy in whirlpools of air and water above me. Lightning splits the sky, an enraged heavenly strobe. It stabs at me with light. Thunder shakes the ground, bellowing in my chest. The icy wind is insistent. A cacophony of shouting, cheering, booing from massive crowds of tattered people swells to painful volume behind me. I am assaulted with noise and violence. I am surrounded, disoriented.

Jesus hangs on a rough wooden cross above me. His body is mangled, gashed horribly, exposed muscles quiver in pain. Streams of blood drip down His body onto the ground in front of me. It is the most terrible sight I have ever seen.

Jesus looks at me. He recognizes me. He says nothing but His eyes pierce my soul. I am transfixed. For a moment the thundering skies and shouts fade into void. I am in a vast space where nothing exists except Christ and my soul. His gaze conveys so much. He knows me. In the midst of being tortured, hung and murdered, He knows me completely, everything about me, every tiny detail, every moment of every hour of my 52 years of life.

I cower in shame.

Underneath the wounded flesh I feel His embrace of impending death. He chooses this. He chooses to remain on that cross every second. He is completely God, completely aware, completely in control of His fate. He can come down from that cross at any moment, instantly end His pain. He chooses to stay there. For me.

I collapse to the ground in shock. I push my face down into the ground. It is foul, clods of hard dirt covered with blood, guts, feces, gruesome. And I am lying in it. The foul earth is nothing compared to the horror of Christ's dying body hanging above me. I can't breathe. My mouth opens in a silent scream of horror.

Mary and Teresa pull me to my feet; their hard fingers bruise my arms. I am a sobbing rag doll. They hold my right hand tightly and push it up to touch Jesus' feet. I pull back but their grips are firm. They are stronger than me. They press my recoiling hand onto the top of His foot.

The instant my fingers touch His toes, electricity blasts into my soul. His love instantly overwhelms me and I willingly push my hand more firmly onto His foot. A hundred men couldn't pull me away from him now. Mary and Teresa release me and step aside. As I gaze up at my beautiful dying Savior, my spirit screams out His name over and over, "Jesus! Jesus! Jesus!"

His torn body is too appalling to behold. I can no longer bear it. I beg Teresa, "I don't want to see Him like this anymore! Please take me away from here!"

She smiles at me. The scene in front of me immediately transforms into the fiery glory of God that I have seen so often before. Its exquisite brilliance engulfs me. As I weep, a voice says, "I will wipe all the tears from your eyes," and a hand softly caresses my face.

Then everything disappears and I am back in my physical room. As I pray, God instructs me to write *everything* down. This is my assignment, to write *all* of these visions down.

PART 1. VISIONS

AUGUST 2019.
WHEN THE VISIONS BEGAN.

I know where I'm going.

I see the light ahead of me.

I'm leaving the darkness behind.

I know peace will soon be mine.

And though I've traveled so far,

And climbed so high,

I know that the heights I will reach

Are far beyond my brightest fantasy,

More perfect than perfection itself,

Miles deeper than the deepest well,

And more exquisite

Than any earthly gem.

I am before the beginning

Of wonderfulness,

Before the beginning

Of beauty,

Before the beginning

Of light…

from "Before the Beginning"
song lyrics by Blue Tapp

I'M NOT CRAZY... MAYBE

I don't want people to think I'm crazy. They will.

I don't want to tell this story. I must.

You might find it difficult to believe. I wouldn't blame you...

~ ~ ~

In August 2019, I began to prayerfully meditate every day. The visions began almost immediately. Everything changed. My goal had been to take more control over my thought life, to learn how to take every thought captive to Jesus Christ. I struggled with racing thoughts. I was hungry for more stillness and peace in my spirit. I wanted to learn how to rest in the Holy Spirit's embrace. Visions were not even on my radar. I had no idea such a thing even existed today. I only hoped that meditative prayer might deepen my relationship with God.

I read a book by Eckhart Tolle about meditation.[1] Tolle's book is not a Christian book. I have no idea of his religious ideologies actually. His book doesn't go there.

---

[1] Tolle, Eckhart. *The Power of Now.* Novato, California: New World Library, 2000

I usually stick to Christian books. I've already wasted too much of my life. I don't have time to read books that don't draw me nearer to God.

I'm not sure even why I read Tolle's book except that God divinely directed it. I had stumbled upon a video interview of him and felt that spiritual nudge. I cracked open his book (well actually fired it up on my Kindle) to see what Mr. Eckhart had to say about meditation. I prayerfully decided to give it a try and intentionally infused my Christian faith into the meditation process Tolle describes.

Tolle explains it as emptying the mind of all extraneous thought chatter to focus only on the now. He calls it being present. I call it meditative prayer. The goal is to be still, to quiet the racing mind and emotions. My intention was to use the stillness to draw nearer to Jesus, to rest in the presence of God.

THE MEDITATION PROCESS

Here is the process I use. I start with several deep breaths, sitting up straight, shoes off, both feet on the floor, with my arms to my sides and hands clasped together in my lap. That first summer I sat outside in our screened in porch behind our old farmhouse to practice.

I slowly contemplate my surroundings... visually examining the contents of our porch... the ornately carved metal fire table in front of me, the faded barnwood boards on our porch walls, the bright ceramic sun and antique iron stars hanging on the wall, the ancient wooden door with wavy glassed windows. I gradually narrow my focus to smaller and smaller fragments, individual nails in the wooden floor, the polished curve of a brass doorknob, the auburn starburst pattern on the doors of our antique gas stove, now emptied of its metal insides and serving only to look pretty on the porch. I do not think about these things. I don't make any mental judgments about what I am looking at. I only observe.

I close my eyes and listen to the sounds of the summer day and methodically unpeel each layer until I am aware of every sound... cars and trucks barreling by, neighborhood dogs barking, birdsongs rising and falling in the humid air, the ever present drone of the katydids, the air conditioner's hum.

I quiet my thoughts and acknowledge the sensations of each moment. I shift my attention inward to my breath drawing in and exhaling out, the blood swishing through my veins, heart beating a rhythm beneath it all.

I become aware of my spirit. I hold out my hand in front of me and close my eyes. How do I know my hand is there? My fingers tingle softly. I concentrate on the tingling and move it up and down my body through my legs into my feet, back up to my chest, down my arms and again into my fingertips. This is my spirit, the eternal part of me. Eckhart Tolle calls it "being." I call it my soul.

If I enter into my meditation with an intentional awareness of God, I always feel His presence. The meditation becomes wordless prayer. Shutting off my brain and tapping into my soul in this way creates space for my spirit to commune with God in a pure, focused manner. It opens a doorway for God to work more powerfully in me than He is able to do during times when I am distracted by all the busyness of my life.

WE ARE NOT OUR THOUGHTS

We think we are defined by our thoughts and beliefs. Really this prattle rattling around in our brains is not much more signicant than our fickle emotions. Both are temporal, fading as they age along with our bodies. Our souls are immortal. Only our souls will remain when death finally claims these terminal bodies of ours.

We think we are our thoughts. We have become addicted to our ever-present thought chatter. It fabricates the narration of our days, critiquing the people around us, noting offenses, bludgeoning ourselves for perceived flaws, worrying about the electric bill, planning our weekend, assembling our shopping lists.

What if we could just make it stop? Stop for a blessed few moments of internal silence? Ten glorious minutes of peace?

It is possible, although difficult to learn. It requires considerable practice. It is possible, and so worth the effort. Taming the incessant babble of our brain is the secret to the deepest joy. It is a key to spiritual awakening and growing closer to God.

I began to sense a great spaciousness during my meditations, as if my consciousness was temporarily released from the confines of my physical body. I could observe my own thoughts and emotions from a detached place of newfound objectivity. I was no longer anxious about potential struggles, no longer offended by perceived insults, no longer easily irritated by daily inconveniences. As my spiritual awareness grew more expansive, the physical me diminished in importance. I became calmer, filled with peacefulness, profound contentment.

I didn't try to make these changes happen to me. They just did.

THE PRESENCE OF GOD

Always during my meditations I was intensely aware of a magnificent loving presence around me and in my thoughts. There is no other way to explain it. It was not me. It was God.

God has been my present companion a million times. Every time I seek, He has met me somehow. Every single time. Always during prayer, or when I listen to haunting music, or when I walk in the woods, or when I gaze at a beautiful sunset. I love these exciting experiences. They feel so glorious, God's embrace.

This was no different. Meditation opened a doorway and God walked in and touched my soul.

I was never at all in control of when or how often these glimpses of glory occurred before. They came when they came… fleeting and rare.

Meditative prayer gave me a method for intentionally seeking out these divine moments. I believe that only God is ever really in control of these sorts of experiences. Much as we would desire it, there simply can't be a "10 Steps to Enlightenment" or "Divine Visions for Dummies." If you ever find such a book sitting on a bookstore shelf, don't waste your money. It doesn't work that way. It can't. I believe God is sovereign. He's in charge of everything in this universe, including each tiny moment of our little lives.

My experience has been that God tends to respond to this practice of presence in some way... often with one of these exhilarating spiritual high experiences. At least God has responded this way to me so far.

At first this was nothing alarming. Again, I've felt these spiritual highs so many times. Most people will recognize the feelings I'm talking about. Most of us have had some version of this happen to us at one time or another. Deja vu. A compelling sensation of wellbeing. A sudden acute feeling of peace. Sound familiar?

LESSONS

Then these strange visions started happening to me, almost every day. It was exciting and fantastic at first. I was giddy with joy.

At first it was just God talking to me, teaching me things.

Even this is something I'd experienced many times in the past, hearing what I believe to be the voice of God. It is often a word of encouragement or discipline. Sometimes a prophecy. Whenever this voice has spoken to me over the years, it has never been wrong.

I am hardly unique in this either. Many people of faith also experience this and would agree that God does indeed choose to *speak* to some people. It isn't usually an audible voice heard with my ears but a deep quiet voice *heard* in my soul. It is strong and authoritative… completely different than any of all the other *voices* I've ever heard in my mind.

God's voice doesn't even always use words. It is more eloquent than human language, more like wordless epiphanies. Sometimes God opens up my mind to understand things in a new way. The new understanding often happens instantaneously, without a verbal explanation, as if God injects the knowledge directly into my soul in little explosions of new awareness. I've since learned that there is actually a word for this phenomenon: locutions. They've actually got a word for it. I guess I'm not the only one who has experienced this.

So God started teaching me things, I would call them lessons, about Himself, about life and truth. Obviously these lessons are difficult to describe using words, since they are, afterall, often wordless. I still try to record everything in my constant journaling. To give you an idea of these, here are a couple of those first lessons from my journal…

What it means to be fallen…
To be *fallen* means that our *natural state* is *imperfect*. We must work to stay close to God. We must always *try* to follow God. It will never just come naturally because following God and being close to God is not our natural state. If we do not actively seek God, the chasm between ourselves and God

grows deeper with the passage of time. The further away from God we descend the more we are filled with great blindness and unhappiness. We feel that we are drowning in a dark pit. Although connecting to God is not our natural inclination in this fallen state, our soul, the eternal part of us, still longs for God. We understand deep within us that without God, we are incomplete. We must only look up and God will immediately reach down to begin pulling us up closer to Himself.

How to truly seek God...
It took me so long to really *find* God even though I was *trying* to seek God most of my life. My *seeking* was too aggressive — too steeped in following religious dogma I grew up with. I was too full of preconceived expectations of what I was going to find that I missed the actual answer. And that is how rigidly following dogmatic beliefs, such as the Pharisees did in the Bible, can blind people to God's voice. God has taught me in my visions that really finding truth sometimes requires a *passive* submissive seeking that holds no expectations — that is completely surrendered to whatever God actually wants to show me. God's voice can be found in the silence... when we quiet our own thoughts and let God commune with our souls *in whatever way He chooses* to communicate with us.

Later in this book I organize these into topics and share much more. This gives an idea of the little *lessons* I learned as I meditated. This was how it all began.

GOING DEEPER.

I'm hungry for illumination
To satiate the blackness in my soul
And I've tasted drops of pure elation
Before waking up again down below

from *"Twenty Four Hours from Depravity"*
song lyrics by Blue Tapp

Here's where it starts getting really freaky.

During my meditations I felt that my consciousness was being transported to some other place outside of my physical body. At first it felt like I was going to a large darkened room. *Room* isn't the right word at all because it felt more like a vast space, too immense to be physically enclosed, although it was too dark to visually confirm this. It was a peaceful place. And I always sensed the presence of God there.

I began to be spiritually transported to this place almost daily during my meditations. I did notice that if I tried too hard to go there, I couldn't. I experienced this only when I intentionally surrendered to whatever God wanted to do with me during my meditation. I couldn't willfully concoct this spiritual journey in my own imagination. It only happened when I relaxed into meditation and cleared my thoughts from my mind. It always had to be God's timing. I was never in control of this. I did find that as long as I would willingly surrender my time and thoughts, God took me there almost every single day. It was quite fantastic and magical.

Over time I could sense a little bit more of what was in that vast space along with me... as if a soft light was gradually turned on. I became aware that the space was filled with other people, thousands, maybe millions or even billions of other humans. I couldn't really see them clearly. They were just shadowy figures in my peripheral vision. I couldn't look directly at them. I could sense their presence more and more precisely with each visit.

Let me stop right here to say that these were *visions,* spiritual perceptions. Were they more than visions? Were these things really happening to me? I don't know. Only God can answer that. It all felt incredibly real to me. This was all a *spiritual* experience rather than physical. One thing I knew for certain though, was that I was really having these visions. They were not simply some wild fantasy I was conjuring up within my own imagination.

These people in my visions, I did not know if these were the souls of human beings who had physically died or were still alive like me. They were benevolent. I sensed only friendliness and warmth from these mysterious creatures. They surrounded me and stood close to me. They appeared to be aware of my presence and welcomed me. I realize this may all sound ominous but it was never a frightening experience in any way. Rather it always filled me with deep peacefulness and utter joy. And always there was this magnificent overpowering sensation of God's presence saturating everything.

I began to understand that I should pray with these people. I felt that God had given us an assignment to pray for the world together. Perhaps many of them had been there praying for the world together for a very long time... decades maybe centuries or longer if these were indeed souls of the departed. I felt as if God was allowing me to join in and participate with these souls in this momentous assignment of praying for the world. No one told me these things. The knowledge was just implanted into my consciousness.

The more I practiced meditating the easier it became to silence my inner thought monologue and enter into deep meditation. Almost daily now God would grab my consciousness and whisk me away to this holy place to pray with all the other souls. My body often physically reacted to the visions. At times my whole body convulsed, not violently like a seizure, more like an extended shiver up and down my body. Occasionally I lost my ability to move — like a temporary paralysis. And I slumped over on my couch. If I had been standing at these times I would have fallen down. Was this *being slain in the spirit*?

My meditations became more intense. I could feel myself holding hands with the souls on either side of me, exchanging energy through our palms. I physically held my hands out beside me and pressed my fingers into my palms and could sense their hands in mine. It is a mystery I cannot explain. I felt in my spirit their hands holding mine. It tingled and I felt the energy of God, the Holy Spirit, coursing through our connected hands.

Other times I held my hands up toward God and I could feel everyone else doing the same motion simultaneously. We all moved concurrently in the spirit like a choreographed dance as if the Holy Spirit moved all of us together in unison. Often I sensed a great brilliant warm light in the middle of our circle, slightly above us. I understood this light to be the *glory of God*.

Other times I saw the earth in the middle of our circle. We all held out our hands toward the earth in unison as we prayed. Sometimes I could see light energy emanating out from our palms and going toward the earth. It felt like electricity tingling down my arms and out of my palms. Normal physical size and space had no relevance in this place, it bent and changed constantly. Sometimes I could move my hands around the earth directly in front of me, caressing it. I felt God's love flowing through me and through all of us into the world.

Often I pressed my palms together in prayer position and felt Holy Spirit power flowing through my palms. I took my shoes off and pressed my feet to the floor and energy surged up from the ground into my feet, through my body. It was all such an electric experience that left me breathless. The electricity tensed up my muscles and occasionally I was even physically sore afterwards.

My meditations became quite physical as I wildly gestured. I became less aware of my actual physical surroundings. I was careful only to meditate in solitude where I would not be observed. Seclusion was of utmost importance. I wanted to feel comfortable, unwatched, and completely free from self-consciousness. I can meditate when my environment doesn't meet these standards if necessary but it is more difficult. I much prefer to be free to move, gesture, dance, kneel, speak, laugh, sing, whatever I feel the Holy Spirit leading me to do. I am careful not to make this any kind performance to display my holiness (as if I had any). This is private time between God and me.

These visions were mostly silent at this point. I did sometimes think words in silent prayer or speak in tongues but usually our prayers had no human language or words. They were all light and energy, visions and sensations.

At times I could feel strong sound vibrations like millions of prolonged harmonizing notes. They seemed to emanate from the air itself. They filled up my mind and body in a magnificent spiritual chorus. It was perceptible only in short bursts like moving a radio dial back and forth between stations. The deeper my meditation, the more I could hear it. I began to hear this song when I walked in the woods. It is God's song of the trees… of the universe… the song of creation praising its Creator.

I shared what was happening to my husband and best friend, Craig. Bless his heart, he told me that he believed me and didn't think I was insane. I think he was telling me the truth. Maybe he is crazy too.

OPENING MY EYES

I had not been able to see any of the other souls in this place distinctly. They were only faint figures moving around me in the twilight. I was very aware of their presence and certain they were there. I could not see any defined features, faces, or colors.

Then one day I was deep in meditation in the place (I will call it *the holy place* from now on), holding hands with the souls on either side of me. I looked to my right and suddenly I could clearly see the smiling mouth of the person standing next to me. It was dazzling — a big wide smiling mouth. It was a bit of an Alice in Wonderland Cheshire Cat experience. I still couldn't see anything else but a dim outline of a body. Now I could see a huge brilliantly illuminated smiling mouth on the face of this soul. It was smiling at me.

I was fantastically shocked… so much so that it zapped me immediately out of my vision and back onto my couch on the back porch where I was physically sitting.

24

I sat there for a long time in a stupor. What did this mean? Who was this? Was it someone I know? I felt like maybe it was. I didn't know who. I had felt so much love and familiarity emanating from that smile.

The next day it happened again, and the next. Now it no longer zapped me out of the vision. I stayed there and observed. I wanted to know who this was. I asked God to show me. And God did. Over the next several days, God gradually revealed to me who was the owner of this radiant smile.

Are you ready for this?

DAD.

The owner of that glorious smile was my dead father. My wonderful funny dad who had died from cancer four years before. My dad who had accepted his terminal sentence with grace and peace and died a mere three weeks after learning of his cancer. He died at home in his bed surrounded by his family. My mother, brother and I cared for him moment by moment during his last three days with us. It was emotionally wrenching but also a divinely beautiful time. My father had deep faith and knew he would so soon be in arms of his beloved Jesus.

On the morning of the day he died, he kept telling us, "Wait… wait… wait… " over and over. We couldn't figure what he was trying to tell us. I had to drive home for something that morning. I begged God through floods of tears during that 40 minute drive to please reveal to us what he was trying to say.

Clearly I heard God's voice respond, "He is not talking to *you*. He is talking to ME." I rushed back to tell my mother and brother what I believed God had told me. We wondered if perhaps Dad was asking God to let him remain with us a little longer. Dad's youngest brother, Mark, was his only sibling who still had not arrived. His other sisters and brother, nieces, nephews, and grandchildren had traveled from all across the country to join us during those last days. Mark was the only one still not there. He was on his way. Of all his siblings, Mark was the one Dad worried about. Mark had led a hard life of drug addiction, incarcerations, and pain. Dad loved him and prayed for him for so many decades.

Mom, Michael and I sat down on Dad's bed and Mom asked him, "Scott, are you asking God to wait?" He nodded yes. She asked, "Are you wanting to wait for Mark to get here?" He nodded emphatically, with more energy than we had seen in the past 24 hours, YES.

Mark finally arrived and we hurried him into Dad's bedroom. When he saw his brother, Dad sat up in bed, the first time in over 24 hours, reached out his arms and pulled his weeping brother into his hug.

Dad died two hours later. Mom, Michael and I stood around him in the moments after his spirit left his body. I smiled up at the ceiling in case his soul might still be lingering there with us. You did it, Dad. You are going home now. You are free.

My dad had come back to me in an extraordinarily vivid dream a year previously and told me he wanted to *take me back with him*. I thought he had been joking in the dream (haha). Are these visions what he had been alluding to? My silly jokester dad who, judging from his enormous smile, was so obviously pleased as punch (as he would certainly be) to see me there.

What did this mean? Could I really commune with the dead? Was this okay? Was this somehow a trick of Satan? Were these shadowy figures demons?

I grew up a Southern Baptist Christian and we were taught that spiritual mediums and fortune tellers and all such things were terribly evil. I believe that often Satan does use such things to connect people to his evil kingdom. Were the things we have been warned about the same as what was happening to me?

I searched the Scriptures but could find no clear message that this was impossible or wrong. Instead I found stories of the dead saints being allowed to visit,[2] the dead being raised again,[3] and Elijah and Moses visiting Jesus.[4]

And then there's this man (himself?) Paul describes as

> ...a man in Christ who fourteen years ago was caught up to the third heaven. Whether it was in the body or out of the body I do not know—God knows. And I know that this man—whether in the body or apart from the body I do not know, but God knows—was caught up to paradise and heard inexpressible things, things that no one is permitted to tell.[5]

---

[2] 1 Samuel 28

[3] Matthew 27:52-53

[4] Matthew 17

[5] 2 Corinthians 12:2-4 NIV

28

I remember reading that passage in the past and wondering what in the world Paul was talking about. Now it sounds remarkably familiar to me.

I also knew from my own extensive experiences with demons growing up (these stories will come later in this book) that demons never work this way. Even when they are disguising themselves as angels of light, as they occasionally do, they are not capable of creating the prolonged euphoric worship of God that I was experiencing. These visions were deepening my love for Jesus. They were causing me to worship God. Demons don't do that.

I took this to prayer, hard soul-wrenching prayer. I asked that if this wasn't from God then take it away. I begged God to protect me from any lies or tricks.

God kept assuring me, in the soft gentle loving way that He does, that this was indeed real, pure and holy. I felt that it delighted God to give me these visions. And they were afterall, visions. I have no way to know if my dad was really interacting with me, or if these were just perceptions, like wakeful dreams, that God put into my mind. Only God knows these things. Either way, I began to understand that God was in control of this. This wasn't my own imagination or some evil demonic trick.

And so after a few weeks of spiritual wrestling, I finally quit fighting it and let myself just go there. The next day when my meditation took me to the holy place, I had a beautiful, emotional reunion with Dad. We hugged and cried and talked for a long time. I could hear him talking to me. I still couldn't see him clearly except for his smile. I could feel his hug and hear his voice in my spirit. He was so excited that I recognized him and so happy to see me. He was so Dad, but a perfect, whole, healthy, joyful version of Dad rather than the frail cancer-ridden Dad I had last physically seen. Thank you, thank you, thank you God for such a sweet glorious experience.

So then after our joyful reunion, Dad and I got back to this business of praying for the world together. Now when I journeyed to the holy place, Dad was always there to my right holding my hand. He would acknowledge me when I got there, squeeze my hand and I would say "Let's do this." and we would pray for the world along with the rest of the other souls in this amazing holy place.

Please understand that I realize how insane this all sounds…

THE SECOND SOUL

I gradually became aware of a second soul always standing to my left, holding my hand and praying with me. I felt that I might possibly know this person as well. So I again asked God to reveal the identity of this second soul. And once again it was eventually divulged to me several days later.

30

It was my long lost Grandma. Dad's mother, Rosemary, who passed away almost two decades before. My plucky spunky sassy Grandma, who always lamented that she wasn't a sweet little old lady like some of the sweet little old ladies at her church. We all loved her just the way she was, quick on the draw with hilarious sarcasm. And oh how she loved us grandchildren. We were her biggest joy. She went into debt every Christmas to shower us with mountains of presents underneath her silvery tinsel bedecked tree. She perhaps didn't make the wisest financial decisions but nothing was too much for her beloved grandkids. She wanted us to have everything she never had. We didn't understand, as children, how difficult her life had been, growing up poor in rural Indiana with a husband absent to fight the Korean War and five children to raise. Any residual sadness she hid deep behind her ready smile and nonstop teasing. Teasing us was her playful love language that my dad, my brother and I all inherited. Thank you, Grandma, for laughter.

How thrilled I was to see her in my visions. Once Grandma's identity was revealed, I was able to talk to her and see her a little more clearly as well. She remained much more shadowy and fuzzy than Dad. I was unable to see her smile or any other feature although I could feel her hand clasping mine and sometimes hear her voice in my spirit. What does this mean? Maybe people who have been gone longer can't appear as clearly? I have no idea the reason. There are so many mysteries here.

Grandma seemed so happy that I recognized her, just as Dad had been. They both listened as I told them about my life now and how Mom and my brother were doing. Perhaps they already knew these things. I asked for their help with my strained relationship with my mother. They comforted and encouraged me.

It went on like this for another week or so. God would bring me into the holy place, I would grab Dad's hand and then Grandma's. We would give each other's hands a quick squeeze and then commence praying for the world. It was our assignment from God. Our glorious divine humbling assignment from God.

I know how insane all of this sounds. This story is just outrageous, completely unbelievable. I never would have predicted these crazy visions. How could any of this really be happening?

I may be bonkers afterall but I promise I am definitely not just making this up. These visions originate from someplace altogether different than my normal imagination. I admit I am a storyteller, a writer. This is unlike anything I have ever experienced before. The stories I *make up* are coming from my own imagination… I know what that feels like. These visions are completely different. Plus remember that they are, afterall, *visions*. Like Paul who describes a man "caught up to paradise and heard inexpressible things, things that no one is permitted to tell," I also do not know "whether it was in the body or out of the body."[6] Was I really seeing my Grandma or only a vision of her, like a dream, from God? Only God knows.

THE HOLY PLACE

One day as I was deep in meditation, I noticed that the air felt cold as I inhaled. I was sitting on my back porch on a humid August day. The actual physical air was very warm. It felt strangely cold as I drew it into my lungs. In my vision, I could see my breath as I exhaled.

I opened my spiritual eyes and found myself standing in a vast lush green canyon surrounded by massive craggy snow-covered mountains. Dad and Grandma were there as were all the millions of other souls. I instantly understood that this breathtaking place was the same holy place I always visited. I had been unable to see it before in the darkness. God allowed me to see it clearly… He turned on the light for me and the human veil was removed from my eyes that day.

I have never in my life seen such a lovely place. The valley floor was covered with gently waving grasses. Several waterfalls cascaded down the mountains and tumbled into a crystal clear river that flowed through the center of the valley. The mountains were treeless, immense craggy rocks jutting up

---

[6] *2 Corinthians 12:2-4 NIV*

steeply from the edges of the canyon with snow blanketed summits. The air was crisp, cool and sweet. The sky was a cloudless luminous blue. The radiant glory of God appeared as a great flaming orb in the center of the enormous circle of souls. God's glory was the only sun illuminating this entire holy place.

And there we were. I could see everyone so much more clearly now. Millions, maybe billions of souls floating slightly above the valley grasses in an endless ring of humanity around the glowing sun of God's glory. I could plainly make out bodies, arms, legs, and heads now. Still there were no distinct faces beyond Dad's smile. This was so much better than before. We grasped each other's hands. We held out our arms toward the sun and praised God together.

And the music… Now I could undeniably hear the cosmic chorus I had heard before only in fragments. Now it was constant and thundering, almost deafening. A billion harmonizing prolonged notes blending together, reverberating through the air and echoing back from the canyon walls. We were singing. The water was singing. The grasses were singing. The sky was singing. God's majestic glory directed it all.

I did not want to ever leave.

Of course I eventually had to return to my mundane physical life. I'm not dead yet. Some day I will get to linger in that enchanted paradise forever. In the meantime, God has granted me the great favor of experiencing this remarkable place if only temporarily. I have no death wish anymore. I love this life God has given me. How marvelous to be offered a glimpse of what I believe is waiting for me after death. I am blessed beyond comprehension. I've returned there many times in my spirit but often it remains dark and shadowy. How wonderful it is when I occasionally get to see it all lit up and magnificent.

DOUBTS

I continue to meditate every day but I don't always go to the holy place. I've discovered that if I try too hard to go there, I don't. If I don't begin by quieting my thoughts, emptying myself of me first, then God doesn't usually take me there. I'm not driving this ship. God is in complete control of it. I have found that if I enter my meditation with total open surrender to whatever God wants to do with that time, He usually responds with a vision… lately. I don't know if this will always happen for the rest of my life or if it is just a season… or frankly if it will happen tomorrow or ever happen again (but I think it will… I hope so). Either way, God's will be done. I will always treasure these amazing memories.

So when I don't go to the holy place, I use that time to pray for my loved ones and other things. Even that sort of prayer has changed for me now. I don't need to use words very much anymore. Language almost feels inferior… as if I'm going backwards to pray with language. This new wordless prayer seems so much more pure, prescient and effective. It is my soul praying rather than my mind. I either pray in tongues or simply visualize the person and in my spirit lift them up to God. Sometimes in the spirit I will see the person lying in front of me with their head and shoulders towards me. I will often hold out my hands and lay hands on their head and shoulders. Sometimes I physically raise my hands and their body is lifted up to God.

There are differing levels of depth to my visions. Sometimes when God does take me to the holy place, it's only very faint and I will shift back and forth between there and here many times throughout my meditation. Other times I go very deep and lose all sense of my actual physical surroundings.

I believe that there is some sort of divine wall between our physical existence and the spiritual realm. I believe that the spiritual world isn't some place far away out in the cosmos. It is always swirling around us, inhabiting the exact same space that we occupy but on another plane, a fourth dimension perhaps. I believe that perhaps my visions are God allowing me to briefly peek through that wall. Maybe sometimes God also allows people who have died, and are now existing in the spirit world, to peek through that wall back into our physical world. If this is true then God, in a mystifying act, has juxtaposed these two miracles in my visions. My glimpses into the spirit realm have coincided with my father and grandmother being offered glimpses back. These are extraordinary gifts God has given to all three of us. Again, it might only be visions that God is showing me, not necessarily something that is really happening, but more of a waking dream, a message that God is showing me. Either way, these visions are marvelous, amazing gifts from God.

I believe that God is really giving me these vision experiences, that I am not making them up in my imagination. Sometimes I doubt. Almost every day I have a little thought shoot through my brain telling me that none of this is real. I must be imagining it all. I must be just absolutely nutso bonkers. Then I'll have another intense vision experience and know with certainty that these are real visions and not imagined. Then again by the end of the day, that tiny hint of skepticism returns.

These suspicions don't alarm me. I would be more worried if I never had these nagging doubts. I need to question my visions. It keeps me humble. The mystery of it all reminds me that I am totally reliant on God for knowing what is real and what isn't. Faith is always like that. If there were some concrete tangible method of proving such things, no faith would be needed. This is the way God has always operated.

TERESA.

Sometimes I feel so alone.

Sometimes I ache for my home.

Sometimes I hear Your haunting song,

Whispered majesties yet to come.

This world can't replace You.

I'll leave it to take You.

You're too good to be true, You

Are the loveliest crazy I ever knew…

"Loveliest Crazy"
song lyrics by Blue Tapp

Just when I thought things couldn't get any weirder…

I began to notice yet another soul during my meditations. Now every time I went to the holy place, Dad would be on my right and Grandma on my left, usually holding my hands. Now sometimes someone else would be standing in front of me. Sometimes I felt this person's hands on my head as they prayed over me. Other times they tightly clasped my hands in front of me, sometimes so firmly it hurt. I thought this must be someone new that God wanted to introduce to me. Who was it? Someone I had known? Another family member? Or someone else? I started asking God once again to reveal their identity to me.

And again God did…

Over the next several days God revealed to me, through little bursts of new knowledge, that this was St. Teresa of Avila, a sainted nun who lived in Spain during the early 1500's. I understood that she was to be my spiritual guide.

How neat.

I knew of Teresa of Avila. I had been briefly interested in various Catholic mystics over a decade before and had read a short biography about her life. She was a prolific writer of books, memoirs and letters and I had attempted to read her most well-known book *"Interior Castle."* I found it difficult to wade through the text (as is often true of 500 year old writings) and quickly abandoned the effort. The biography had been very interesting to me though. I was inspired by her tenacious work ethic as she founded many monasteries for Carmelite nuns and friars in Spain through great hardships and ill health. I had also been intrigued by her raptures. These were vision experiences she often had, during which it is told that she occasionally even levitated. My interest had waned. I hadn't thought about her in many years.

Now I believe I may have actually *met* her, or had a vision of her, at least.

And God has apparently *assigned* her as my spiritual guide.

Wow.

As was the case with both Dad and Grandma, once her identity was revealed, I was able to see her more clearly and interact with her in my visions. I could see her face and hands. She wore a thick coarse black and white habit. Her face was ancient, a roadmap of deep intersecting wrinkles with piercing dark eyes and a stern mouth. Her hands were strong with knobby arthritic knuckles and protruding veins. Not exactly how I would have predicted a soul in this holy place would look. She was afterall over 500 years old!

Curiously I could see much more of my new guide than I could see of either Dad or Grandma. I could still only see Dad's smile and couldn't really see Grandma at all. They both remained vague shadowy figures. What a mystery this all is.

I realized that my visions might be similar to Teresa's raptures (although I haven't levitated yet haha). Could God have paired us because of this? I hoped maybe these visions of Teresa could help me understand what was happening to me and to navigate wisely through these strange experiences.

Teresa and I started talking a lot in the visions. I could hear her clearly. Her voice was thin and elderly but forceful. At first I felt quite intimidated to be in her presence. She often seemed impatient with how far I have yet to go, how much I have to learn. She reprimanded me when I lost my focus. She held my hands so tightly it was painful at times. I imagine in her life she would have been reluctant to take on someone like me as her protege, so selfish and worldly compared to the willfully impoverished nuns she usually mentored.

She also called me "child." She often placed her hands on my head and prayed for me. I began to sense a great compassion and tenderness within her as the visions progressed. Underneath her harsh exterior I felt an intense compassion. I grew to love her fiercely. She was no-nonsense, spunky, feisty, intense… She was the perfect guide for me.

She taught me many things in the visions. She told me that when the enemy puts thoughts into my head I should laugh at him. It completely diffuses his power. She also taught me so much about obedience to God and to human authorities. She said "Obedience brings strength."

I found myself insatiably curious to read everything Teresa wrote, all 30,000 pages of her published writings, books, memoirs and letters. I started again with *Interior Castle*. This time I devoured it.[7] I was fortunate to find a very accessible translation. Just reading it often catapulted me into my own visions… Her descriptions of the various rooms in our spiritual interior castles now seemed so astonishingly familiar.

---

[7] Teresa of Avila, Saint. Trans. Mirabai Starr. *The Interior Castle*. New York: The Berkley Publishing Group, 2003

After I finished *Interior Castle,* I read her first autobiography, and her second and third, then her books and finally all of her letters. It took me a year and a half, but I read every word. I did not always understand the translated 500 year old Spanish. Still I found it filled with countless gems.[8]

How wonderful and divine that God began giving me these vision experiences first and then brought Teresa to help make sense of it. This is one of so many proofs to me that I am not imagining all of this. This turned around order is exactly how God usually works with me. First I have the raw, unexplained experience. Then something happens to clarify the situation. Perhaps it is similar to a spoken prophecy in tongues that is followed by the interpretation as practiced in charismatic churches. I believe this is for my own benefit. It proves to me that I didn't just hear about something and then imagine that very same thing happening to me. When the event happens to me first it is completely outside of my realm of experience, not a conjured up memory, or anything I have ever heard of. It is something so outrageous that I know it did not originate from my own limited imagination.

So it went on like that for a couple of weeks… Dad to my right, Grandma to my left, sometimes Teresa in front of me holding my hands, praying anointing over me, teaching me. When Teresa was not there, Dad, Grandma, and I went back to praying for the world together.

---

[8] Aeterna Press. (Ed.). *Saint Teresa of Avila Collection.* London: Aeterna Press, 2016

It was marvelous. I was loving these magical vision experiences.

WRITE THIS DOWN

Then I was given my own assignment. It started as a gentle nudging, a suggestion from God and Teresa to "write all of this down."

Okay okay I promised. I would definitely write all of this down some day.

"Write all of this down NOW." The message became more insistent about this day after day.

I kept not writing anything down, although it became increasingly clear that I was being instructed to do so. I had a reason to hesitate... *who in the world was supposed to ever read this?* I didn't *want* anyone to read it. Besides Craig (who says he believes me, bless his sweet heart), I had told no one else yet about these insane experiences. Who would ever believe me? They would think I was crazy. Possessed by demons. I might lose friends. No, I most definitely did not want to record any of this. Writing it down meant someone someday might read it and I didn't want anyone to ever know about it. I was scared.

In the visions God and Teresa kept commanding me to write. One day Teresa, sounding exasperated, told me, "Why should I even talk to you if you won't be obedient?"

Both Teresa and God stopped talking to me. I could no longer go to the holy place. Nothing. No visions at all. Total silence for days. I had to obey…

I purchased a nice blue leatherbound journal and a set of fancy pens and started the task of writing it all down.

Now when I sat down to meditate, God and Teresa would tell me "Write! Write! Write!" And so I would write.

I started from the beginning of when the vision experiences started happening and prayed that God would remind me of everything I should write down.

God did.

I wrote.

After about a month of this I went to my prayer place on my porch and begged God to let me spend some time with them that day. I missed them. All I had been doing was writing writing writing. I hadn't had a vision in over a month.

God said okay. I was immediately jettisoned to the holy place with Dad and Grandma and all the millions of other souls. This particular vision was instantly at the highest intensity level, blindingly bright and deafening. Visions of this intensity are physically painful. It seems as if the pain originates from the blazing fireball that is the glory of God, the only sun illuminating everything there much more brilliantly than our own physical sun. God's glory is so powerful that it burns sharply into my soul. It hurts. At the same time it is exhilarating, an exquisite pain that I don't want to ever end.

It did stop after maybe ten minutes. I was abruptly transported back to my porch. In the spirit I could see Teresa, Dad and Grandma staring at me.

"Well…" Teresa said, "Are you happy? Now go write!"

So I wrote.

PART 2. BACK TO THE BEGINNING

1970. MY DEMON. MY JESUS.

On this day I feel I've reached
The bricks in the wall
At the end of a way.
Speak to the darkness
Inside of me.
Push it down and away.

from "My Demon"
song lyrics by Blue Tapp

I'm no stranger to the supernatural. I was 52 years old when I first wrote these words for this book in the year 2019. My half century of life has been filled with many *strange* things.

I began having night terrors when I was very little — maybe three or four years old. I often woke up screaming and shaking. My parents attempted to console me but I was too young then to describe my nightmares to them. I remember them though — shadowy horrors. No visuals. Just blackness combined with intense fear, inescapable doom, and muffled voices. I had no idea what any of this meant. It was terrifying.

Years later my Dad told me of an experience he had during that time, in the early 1970s. He became interested in the subject of demons and started reading books about them. It became a bit of an obsession.

One night after all of us (me, my little brother, and Mom) had gone to bed, he was downstairs in the den reading one of his demonology books. He felt an evil presence enter the den and instantly he had an epiphany. This obsession about demons was dangerous. He needed to end this now. At that very moment, a door upstairs (where we were all sleeping) slammed shut. The house shook and then was silent. Dad's hair stood on end. He was afraid to move.

Finally he put down his book and came upstairs to check on us, turning on lights as he went, terrified to be alone in the darkness. He found us all sleeping soundly in our bedrooms so he crawled into bed with mom and tried to sleep.

After that night he disposed of his demonology books and never delved into the subject again.

My night terrors began during that same time period, perhaps soon after this. I think that might have been the night that *she* entered into my life. Maybe she was trying to attach to my Dad. His rejection of her closed (literally slammed) a door. Maybe she then found a more vulnerable target… little innocent four year old me.

She was a demon. She was present in my thoughts during my entire childhood into adulthood. I don't remember a time of my early life without her. She was always there — talking to me, yelling at me in my head, telling me lies, making me feel crazy. She showed me pictures in my mind of terrible things, of people being murdered, tortured and mutilated — things I knew I had never really seen — things I knew weren't coming from my own imagination. And her voice was very distinctly not the voice of my own thoughts. She was not me. She was an intruder in my own mind.

TO BE OPPRESSED BY A DEMON

So what is it like to be oppressed by a demon? I believe many people are demonically oppressed today. Some realize it. Others have no idea.

Those who believe in Jesus and in the Bible must at least consider the possibility that demons exist. In every town Jesus visited, he cast out demons. He didn't send people to psychiatrists or give them prozac or counsel them. He cast demons out of them. Jesus most certainly believed that demons were real. If that many people were oppressed by demons way back then, in every small town he visited, how many more people are tormented by demons today?

I believe that many people who suffer from depression, bi-polarism, schizophrenia, psychosis and other mental illnesses are actually oppressed by demons. Maybe not always, but oftentimes. Certainly this is often true of people who *hear voices* as I did. Modern psychiatry has no understanding of the spirit world. It is completely ill-equipped to confront the spiritual condition. This is one of the great tragedies of our current anti-depressant addicted depression culture. So many people seek their cure in a pill bottle. Demonic oppression cannot be fixed with pills.

So this was part of my childhood. The scary dreams. The fears. The screaming voice in my head. The confusion. The darkness.

Another part of my childhood was filled with great lightness and comfort. While my demon was trying to destroy me, I on the other hand, was falling deeply in love with Jesus.

I grew up in an old-timey Southern Baptist church. I loved learning Bible stories in Sunday School and singing old gospel hymns in church. I loved listening to the tinny harmonies of the little old ladies and men singing in the pew behind me. I loved my illustrated Children's Bible and read it cover to cover repeatedly. I won a little heart bracelet in Sunday School for memorizing all the names of the books of the Bible. I wore it every day. I was so excited when I *prayed the sinner's prayer* at six years old with my mom and dad to become a Christian. The next day I ran into my first grade class and excitedly exclaimed to my teacher "Ms. Paula! Ms. Paula! I became a Christian!" (That was back when it was okay to talk about such things in public school.)

As I grew up, these two conflicting forces constantly fought for my allegiance — my demon and Jesus Christ. I existed amidst this ever present tension. And my youth was filled with drastic swings between the two.

Always I felt such joy and sweetness when I sought Jesus. It always felt like coming home. I never doubted the existence of God and Jesus. I always believed that God knew me. I *knew* that Jesus loved me and was pursuing me. I felt it. I sensed God's presence whenever I looked for Him. He was perpetually present.

As I entered the angsty teenage years, my demon hit me with her full destructive power. She saw her opportunity within my growing self-consciousness and declining self esteem. Her attacks were relentless.

I was a shy, awkward teenager with buck teeth and glasses. We moved all the time, almost every year. So I never had any friends. I was bullied and picked on. It was a recipe for catastrophe. I flung myself headlong into all the things desperately unhappy kids do these days to feel accepted — drugs, sex, rebellion — I would do any stupid thing I thought might make people like me. I plummeted into terrible depression. My demon's quest to destroy me was working. She was throwing a full-blown victory party within my tortured misery.

SWINGS

The swings continued.

God was always tugging on my heart, gently pulling me back to Himself, my first love. I could feel the presence of the Holy Spirit and longed to return into communion with Him.

My demon was always there as well, screaming at me in my thoughts… pushing me in the other direction — into depression, self-pity, self-harm, suicidal thoughts and self-hatred. She was louder.

I would go to a summer youth retreat and have an intimate Jesus experience which felt so wonderful and pure. Then I would run off with one of the guys in the youth group and mess around behind the bunkhouses. These were scurrilous, meaningless physical encounters that left me feeling dejected and humiliated. My shame would drive me away from God again.

Each swing made me feel more despicable. My demon convinced me that following after God was pointless. I could never be good. Every time I ran away further and harder. I was a mess, out of control, desperately searching for acceptance and love in places where it could never exist. My demon had my soul wrapped around her icy fingers.

Not surprisingly, people with demons attract other people with their own demons. I was drawn to the bad kids, the kids who skipped school, drank alcohol, and smoked pot. I wanted them to like me and I would do anything to fit in. I wasn't really very "cool" and didn't fit in with the bad kids either. I didn't dress the right way or wear my hair the right way and I was bumbling and shy. Adult me realizes how silly and unimportant all of those things are. Teenage me was devastated.

SCHOOL

I was a trainwreck throughout most of high school, hanging out with the wrong kids, having careless sex, experimenting with various drugs. My relationship with my parents degraded into chaos. They had no idea what to do with me. I ran away from home repeatedly.

Luckily I was booksmart and through all the insanity I kept a near perfect grade point average and graduated from high school early with honors. So at least there was one good thing during this crazy time in my life. I always had a strong drive to excel intellectually and succeed in my education. I equated academic success with freedom. *Freedom* was always my driving goal. Educational success meant more job or college choices and escape from my parents.

I began attending community college working toward a degree in fine arts. It was there that I met Jeremy, a fellow art major, who I dated for several years. He was cute and funny but besides that didn't have much going for him. He wasn't very motivated, couldn't keep a job, hated most everyone, and had a fascination with death. Twenty years later he would have been a classic goth kid. Now he was just an anti-social weirdo... a lot like me. And we were instantly drawn to each other.

It didn't take long for me to realize that we had something else in common. He had a demon too. And not just one demon but a bunch of them.

Our demons seemed to get stronger the more we were together — our connection to each other seemed to supernaturally feed them.

Jeremy suspected his demons existed before I met him. He could hear their angry voices and feel their eerie company. After we began comparing notes it became clear to us what was happening. Our increasing awareness of them also seemed to make them stronger, as if our thoughts provided them some sort of spiritual energy.

Some of Jeremy's demons started coming home with me. I began to be able to see them. The first time I actually saw a demon, I was in the shower and sensed its icy presence. A dark shadowy entity floated above me near the ceiling, glaring at me with glowing green eyes. My own demon was always inside my head. Jeremy's demons swam through the air and slowly coiled around us like ghastly demonic snakes.

I could see them often after this — ghostly figures swimming through the air, often at night. Occasionally I could see their bright green shining eyes. I didn't try to resist them. By this point I had resigned myself to my own demonic companion. She had convinced me that trying to draw near to God was futile. I felt sick comfort in her constant company. After I stopped fighting her, she changed towards me as well. Her enraged shrieking accusations turned to alluring promises of popularity and success. She now made me feel strong and powerful. I became quite fascinated with her and wanted to learn more. I incorporated demons into my drawings. My artwork was filled with dark creeping figures in every corner.

Jeremy and I weren't complete idiots. We did understand the demons were bad. We knew the things they told us were probably lies. We knew that they hated us. We were somewhat afraid of them but were still extremely curious about them. The power that they promised us was intoxicating even if we suspected it was all a lie. So we didn't try very hard to make them go away. And our preoccupation with them made them grow ever stronger.

I remembered some spiritual warfare lessons I had learned in church and when the demons felt too threatening I verbally claimed "the power of the blood of Jesus Christ." As trite as it sounds, saying this always seemed to hold power over them. It weakened them. They almost always left us immediately whenever I said "the blood of Jesus" outloud. This was a power I had over them that Jeremy did not possess. His words seemed to hold no authority. He asked me to say the words to make them leave us when we were overwhelmed.

1990. DEMONS.

This is my demon, my demon.
She's bloodsworn to kill my soul.
Drag me down underground,
Drowning in mud and water.
Come back home all alone,
Just a box of rocks in the ground…
In the ground.

from "My Demon"
song lyrics by Blue Tapp

They took it too far one night. I was spending the night at Jeremy's house when his parents were out of town. We both still lived with our parents; we were only teenagers.

As we slept that night, without warning a scream pierced through the midnight silence. We lurched awake, muddled with sleep and sat up in bed, confused. Everything was in slow motion, as though we were swimming in syrup. The room was bathed in an orange pulsing glow that illuminated Jeremy's face.

Gibberish erupted out of Jeremy's open mouth, a strange foreign tongue neither of us knew. He looked at me wide-eyed as he babbled. He couldn't stop the bizarre words. In slow motion he looked toward the orange light and pointed beyond the end of the bed. Flames lapped up the window curtains from the top of his desk. The entire corner of the room was on fire. The scream that woke us was the wailing fire alarm. We sat there staring at the flames in paralyzed stupor.

Suddenly, inexplicably the trance was broken. Time moved at normal speed again. Jeremy jumped up, grabbed his blanket, and smothered out the fire. It happened so fast. We stood there wordless, shocked, breathing heavily, trying to digest what had just occurred.

We carefully surveyed the room. The curtains were scorched but little else was burned. It was difficult to believe that all those flames had caused such scant damage.

Jeremy returned to bed and we layed there quietly in the darkness, hearts still pounding.

We both felt it when it arrived. A monstrous evil presence slowly filtered into the room and rolled through the thick air above us. Dark weight pressed down onto us. My blood turned to ice. Jeremy was lying on his side facing me, arms around me. We both knew it was there. Jeremy quietly begged me, "Make it go away. Please make it go away."

I was lying on my back with eyes closed, afraid to open them. I knew he was there, right above me, crushing his vile weight down into my chest. This was the most powerful horrifying evil

I had ever felt, a night terror come to life. The feelings of doom, the crippling fear, the helplessness, it all came back to me.

I pried open my eyes. There he was. He was massive, heavy, an immense shadow pushing down on top of us. His flaming green eyes were only inches from mine, searing into my mind. He whispered low, ominous, dark secrets, moaning in a chilling vernacular directly into my shrinking soul.

I opened my mouth to speak "the blood of Jesus Christ." My throat was paralyzed. Nothing would come out. My tongue felt thick, dead weight in my mouth. Painfully, I pushed out the words "I claim the blood of Jesus Christ… I rebuke you demon by the power of the blood of Jesus Christ…" I spoke it over and over again, louder and bolder with each repetition. Gradually we felt the pressure ease as the demon slowly began to fade away. The air thinned and the constricting weight lifted. We could breathe easily once again. The night became still and silent.

We hugged each other tightly and cried together. It was one of the most terrifying things we had ever experienced.

It was incredibly tame compared to things that were yet to come…. only not with Jeremy.

Jeremy's family moved away soon after this and our relationship ended. I've lost contact with him so I have no idea what has become of him. I pray that he has found freedom from his demons.

SPEAKING IN TONGUES

I graduated from community college with an Associates in Fine Arts and transferred to Southeast Missouri State University to work on a B.A. in English Literature. This was my chance for a fresh start. Time for an upswing back to my first love, Jesus. I sought out the Christian students, got involved in the Baptist Student Union and later joined Chi Alpha — a charismatic Christian fraternity outreach of the Assembly of God Church. I got very involved in the Assembly of God Church and made friends there.

My first encounter with charismatic Christianity had been years earlier at one of those non-denominational charismatic mega-churches that grew popular back in the 1980s. A friend from my youth group had invited me. I had been shocked the first time this Southern Baptist girl witnessed people speaking in tongues publicly. People all around me were yelling out strange words, waving their arms around wildly, dancing in the aisles. No one had warned me about this. I wasn't prepared for the insanity and found it frightening. I had walked out of the church in a panic. What in the world was that all about?

60

I was intrigued…. teenager me was disillusioned with the dry legalism of my Southern Baptist roots. Here was something new and exciting. So I went back and kept going. At this church there was a big emphasis on *being baptized in the spirit* and they taught that the *only* proof of this was speaking in tongues *(I do not now believe this is sound doctrine)*. There were two groups there — the baptized who loudly demonstrated their status by yelling out in tongues during worship, and the unfortunate non-baptized of lesser faith who prayed quietly to themselves.

Well of course I wanted to get this exciting gift for myself. I tried and tried to make sounds and speak in tongues but I just couldn't do it. They had teachers who would try to *train* people to speak in tongues by repeating phrases like "Gotta Hava Honda" over and over. I think this is really silly now but at the time I was blinded by my desire to join the baptized favored ones.

One Sunday, special speakers visited the church to teach people how to speak in tongues. During the service they told everyone who wanted the gift of tongues to come to the front of the church. Hundreds of people stampeded down the aisles. This was a mega-church; there were thousands of people there. The energy in the sanctuary was palpable. People practically jumped over pews to get down to the front. I went down too, just as excited as everyone else. Finally to become one of the baptized, the elite. They said they would give us a cue, and we should just open our mouths and make noise and the Holy Spirit would take over. They also told the rest of the church members, the chosen ones who were already baptized, to start speaking in tongues at their cue *(good backup plan)*.

I was standing at the front surrounded by hundreds of other people. The excited fervor was electric. We couldn't wait. And then then they gave the cue... and I opened my mouth...

...nothing happened.

I stood there with my mouth open. No one else around me was speaking in tongues either. We all just stood there with our mouths open, looking around, confused. So many others in the church jabbered loudly in tongues that no one noticed how many of us stood there in silence.

That was an epiphany for me. This whole premise was scammy. If God wanted me to speak in tongues, He would arrange it in His timing, His way. No hype or training was necessary. I pushed through the crowd and went back to my seat and many others did the same. The speakers exclaimed what a glorious thing had just happened. I knew it wasn't true. After that I didn't worry about getting this gift of tongues anymore. I quit asking for it and didn't bother feeling jealous of those who had it.

I *did* actually start speaking in tongues much later after I wasn't going to that church anymore. I wasn't trying to speak in tongues or even thinking about it when it happened. One day I was sitting in my room alone praying, and tongues just flowed out of my mouth. I couldn't even stop it. I spoke in tongues off and on for the rest of that day. I have always been able to do it ever since.

For decades I just thought of tongues as an insignificant little gift that was interesting but useless. I never really understood the purpose of it. Now I believe it is a sign from God to us and much more. It is a unique communication method that God allows us to pierce through the spiritual veil. It is our spirit, rather than our mind, praying to God. Now I understand that it is such a beautiful gift. I am disappointed that this wonderful gift is so misunderstood and abused.

So there I was in college orchestrating my fresh new start, ready for some exciting charismatic church services. I dove right into the Assembly of God church life and got very involved. I joined the worship team at Chi Alpha and participated in church events several times a week, bible studies, worship services, outreach ministry events. I was all in. I was on another spiritual upswing and it felt fantastic.

FIRST DELIVERANCE

During my college years I experienced my first deliverance from my demon. She was still there in my mind, although she had grown much quieter since Jeremy had moved away. Every once in a while she thrusted some barb at me… some lie about how stupid I was or how silly all these new Christian friends were. Most of the time she was silent, planning future attacks, I suppose, waiting for the right time to strike.

I was at a prayer meeting and for some reason she became very agitated and started yelling at me. I have no idea what instigated the onslaught. This was the first time this had happened since at college and I wasn't prepared for the unexpected attack. She didn't speak words, but just shrieked louder and louder in a hideous gutteral howl in my mind. I began to sob quietly.

Others in the room sensed that something was wrong. They all gathered around me, layed their hands on my back and began to pray for peace and deliverance.

The more they prayed, the louder she screeched. It became very painful. I wept loudly. My body shook. They prayed more intensely. She wailed even louder and my body convulsed in a seizure. The pain was agonizing, as if every cell of my body was going to explode. I was lying on the floor now. They prayed louder. She shrieked more vehemently. Everything crescendoed into insanity…

Then suddenly, in my spirit, a door slammed shut. Everything was abruptly silent and still. I laid quietly on the floor. At peace.

She was gone.

I was free.

She didn't return for over a decade.

1997. DEATH.

This crazy girl,
She's in my head.
This crazy girl,
She wants to be dead.
But she's killing me instead.
I hold onto the reins
Of her lunatic chains.
I'm feeling myself slip.
And I'm losing my grip...

from "Crazy Girl"
song lyrics by Blue Tapp

Life started just rolling along. I dated a guy I met at college and we eventually got married. He began attending the Assembly of God Church and Chi Alpha meetings with me and we were very involved there.

We both started to grow increasingly uncomfortable with some of their teachings — particularly their name-it-claim-it ideology and prosperity teachings. Some of their ideas didn't jive very well with the Bible, in our opinion. The leaders ridiculed anyone who disagreed with them and the members ostracized people who visited other churches. It started to feel very cultish to us. We eventually stopped going. We tried a few other churches but nothing clicked. So we stopped trying.

I spent a couple of years just coasting along without really seeking God in my life at all. My demon was gone now. I could just be another typical spiritually-unaware person sleepwalking through life like most everyone else around me.

I graduated with an M.A. in English Literature and began working on a Ph.D. in Rhetoric and Composition. I excelled in college. I taught freshman composition throughout my graduate studies and was selected by the department to teach other graduate assistants how to teach. I immersed myself in my work and education. I loved it. Education was my passion. Education became my new church.

However things at home weren't going as well. After four years our marriage was falling apart. We had been so young and naive, in our early twenties when we had married. Getting married had just seemed like the thing to do. We were not mature enough to understand how to make a relationship succeed. We both changed a lot in four years. Our church attendance had been a commonality that we had now lost. As I delved ever deeply into school, we drifted further apart. He flunked out of college and had trouble keeping a job which frustrated me. He was a nice guy, and a good friend. We just weren't compatible mates. I grew increasingly miserable with our relationship. I wasn't honest with him about this as I should have been. I felt guilty about my waning affection and withdrew into myself. I did not handle things wisely.

I left him without warning. I took my stuff and left. It was a horrible thing for me to to do to him and he didn't deserve it. I broke his heart and I am terribly sorry that I did that. I'm not making any excuses. Leaving him that way was dreadful and wrong and I knew it. But I did what I did. I cannot change the past.

I've lost contact with him but I pray that he has found happiness. For his own sake, I hope that he has found it in his heart to forgive me for the terrible thing I did to him all those years ago. I wouldn't blame him if he could not.

DEPRESSION

I stupidly got into another relationship. He was an angry guy, physically and emotionally abusive. I was guilt-ridden about leaving my husband and thought I deserved the beatings. So I stayed in the relationship and descended into despair. I dropped out of my beloved school without finishing my Ph.D. and plunged into a deep suicidal depression that lasted six long years.

I lived with that monstrous man for a hellish year. We ran a sound system business together and he controlled everything, our money, vehicles, apartment, our activities and social life. He was acutely jealous and separated me from my remaining friends. He thrived on conflict. I wasn't a fighter but he would lash out at me, verbally pushing until I finally responded in defense. Then he hit. I was isolated, beaten physically and emotionally. I lost all passion for anything. I hated myself for getting into this situation. I lost my will to live.

And then I thought I found a way out. An old acquaintance from years before contacted me. She invited me to move out to New York City to help her with an art business she was starting.

I couldn't get out there fast enough. I secretly sold anything I could pawn, left most of my stuff and escaped. I packed up a mini UHaul with a few belongings and ran away from the monster… to another crazy mess.

The business deal turned into a catastrophe. My friend and I had a falling out and I was then stuck in New York City with no place to stay, no vehicle, and very little money. Things had quickly gone from hell to worse….

I found a tiny run down apartment above a coffee shop in Rutherford, New Jersey for $600 a month (almost twice what my nice two bedroom apartment had cost back in Missouri). I got a job working as a vet tech at a nearby veterinary hospital. It was the only thing I could find within walking distance. So there I was with a Masters degree and almost a Ph.D. in English cleaning dog crap out of cages for minimum wage. It was very humbling.

Honestly, in retrospect, it wasn't all that bad. I love animals and I actually enjoyed a lot of parts of the job. I got to assist with surgeries and other procedures and learned a lot. If I hadn't been absolutely crippled by raging depression, I could have toughed it out, looked for a better job, and made a life for myself there.

I had never recovered emotionally from the guilt I felt over leaving my husband. My religious parents had publicly disowned me when I divorced him. They came to divorce court and sat with my husband and never tried to reach out to me in any way. It was painful. So I couldn't ask them for help. I had no friends in New York. I had no support group whatsoever. I was completely isolated. I wasn't mentally or emotionally strong enough at the time to deal with this difficult life situation. I was horribly depressed and I wanted to die.

I'M BACK

If all that wasn't challenging enough, my long lost companion, my demon, returned.

I was sitting alone one evening, drinking in my apartment looking out the open window onto the bricklined courtyard below. It was a cool spring night. I was on my way to drunkeness. She floated in with the breeze and her familiar voice whispered, "I'm back."

70

And she was, along with all of her lies and hatred and screaming at me in my own head. She had been gone for many years, waiting on the outskirts of my life for her opportunity to pounce. My prolonged depression carved out a doorway for her to casually waltz right back in.

Her arrival broke me. I was trapped with my enemy, a bait dog in a cage with a snarling wolf. I felt doomed. To my depression scarred mind, death seemed the only possible escape.

SUICIDE

The first time I tried to kill myself, I stole a surgical blade from the vet hospital and cut into my arm. I cut deep — so deep the skin laid apart on either side of the cut, leaving gaping holes of open veins deep down into my arm. Blood was everywhere, all over me, the floor, soaking into my blanket. Surely this would do it. I drank myself into a wine coma.

The next morning I woke up with a splitting hangover and dried blood all over. How could I have cut so deeply and not bleed to death? Years before, while donating blood, I had passed out and gone into convulsions. The red cross workers brought me back quickly but I'd never forgotten that experience. I thought it would be an easy way to go. I was wrong.

The cavernous hole in my arm needed to be stapled up at a clinic. They asked me if I wanted to be admitted to the psyche ward. Why not? I hadn't ever tried that before. Maybe it would help. So I checked myself in, turned in my shoelaces, was assigned a small plain bed, and spent the next three days there.

It was there I learned that I was not crazy. I was the sanest one there. Some of the folks there were undeniably certifiably insane… sit in the corner rocking back and forth screaming at the wall bonkers. One girl was getting shock therapy treatment. I didn't even know they still did that. Another girl had tried to commit suicide by cutting off her own head with a dull little knife. She didn't get very far with that plan.

The psych ward stint helped me in a way. I found myself trying to encourage some of the others in there with me. They seemed so sad and hopeless. I sang to them and tried to get them to smile. It was good to focus on others. My life wasn't so bad afterall.

I had no insurance so they wouldn't keep me any longer than three days which was good, I guess, because people with good insurance seemed to have trouble getting out. Some of them had been there a very long time. Some of them would probably stay there forever.

DEATH

The depression was far from gone. I returned to my lonely apartment and had now lost my job. I missed half a week of work without giving any notice and someone had found out about the missing surgical blade. They obviously could not let me come back. Any fragile flame of newfound perspective I had gained in the hospital was quickly snuffed out. I still desperately wanted to die. And now I had no income or way to pay my rent. Homelessness loomed inevitably. I had fallen into a deep black pit and again couldn't see any other way out other than suicide.

I was determined not to fail the next time.

I swallowed the handful of sleeping pills that terrible night in my apartment and waited to die…

"Wake up! Wake up!" my four angelic visitors implored me. Their urgent pleas penetrated my drugged oblivion. They spoke directly into my mind, their voices pushed further and further into my consciousness.

"Wake up! Call for help!"

They were so beautiful, luminous in the darkened room. Their shimmering robes silently swayed around their feet. They stared intently at me without blinking, without expression.

"Wake up! Call for help! Call 911!"

Maybe I didn't really want to die.

I slowly crawled across the floor and punched the numbers into my old landline phone. "Hello what is your emergency?"

I died that night. My disembodied spirit floated through hospital corridors. I watched as ER medics pounded on my chest to restart my stilled heart.

God had a different plan.

ALIVE

I woke up in the hospital a couple of days later sore, confused, tubes up my nose, wrists shackled to the bed.

Alive.

I was mad to still be alive at first. I was such a failure that I couldn't even kill myself correctly. A priest asked if he could pray for me and I said no. This time when they tried to check me into the psyche ward I refused. What for? What's the use? I didn't want any help. No one could help me.

I was in the hospital for two days falling in and out of consciousness. I clearly remembered the angels, and the woman in the waiting room holding the baby. It all seemed so real. At first I absolutely believed those things had all taken place. They seemed more real than anything else.

As my muddled thoughts slowly cleared, I realized that I couldn't have *really* physically been in that waiting room or kissed that baby. What had happened?

They released me from the hospital and I tried to put the pieces of my broken life back together.

I called my parents, tail between my legs, prodigal daughter in the pigsty. When I told them what had happened they reluctantly agreed to let me come home. Hope. I wouldn't be homeless on the streets afterall. So I rented another mini UHaul truck with my dwindling funds, packed it with my few belongings and my little Siamese cat and drove across the country back to St. Louis.

1998. BACK HOME.

I used to think that it would take a razor,
Steel on flesh,
To make it all turn out right,
Carving out my masterpiece
In skin and blood and bone.
But not tonight.

The pills went down so easy
With just a little water
Inside of this liquid life,
Under surface.

I want to pull back out and up
Above all of this,
Just like watching a movie.
I'm looking down
At all the world below.
But I can't go.

from "Electric"
song lyrics by Blue Tapp

One would think that having angels come to save me would have been an amazing life-changing spiritual experience that would draw me back to God.

It wasn't. I was emotionally numb and raw, still depressed and oppressed by my demon, and now facing the daunting task of restarting my life in St. Louis at 30 years old.

I began a series of temporary jobs, usually involving building computer databases which I had recently taught myself to do. I was good at it and kept steady work.

I was no longer suicidal. I had experienced death. I didn't want to do that again. I was still depressed and vulnerable and that scared me. So I began seeing a psychiatrist. After hearing my story, she prescribed a cocktail of anti-depressants, mood stabilizers and sleeping pills. Yeah that's right… she prescribed sleeping pills to someone who had overdosed on sleeping pills.

I spent the next three years in a prescribed functional chemical fog.

GEOFFREY

I met Geoffrey on one of those new fangled (at the time) internet dating sites. He was good looking, smooth talking and weird. I like weird. I'm weird too. We started dating.

It didn't take long for me to realize that he had an entourage of his own demons. As with Jeremy, they began to interact with my demon.

Geoffrey's demons were much more powerful than mine or Jeremy's. They affected physical objects. His house was *haunted*. Lights mysteriously turned off and on. Scarey noises came from the television when it was turned off. Streetlights blinked off when he walked close to them.

People, strangers, inexplicably reacted to him in strange ways… yelling at him for no reason, spontaneously telling him macabre stories while they stood in line next to him. One guy came up to him in a grocery store and said, "You're one of THOSE people, aren't you?" He told me many disturbing stories about people he knew dying in mysterious ways. The guy took creepy to a whole new level. I should have run away from him as fast as possible. He was cute, and did I mention a smooth talker? I was still young, stupid, and curious….

One of the many eerie things I witnessed happened at a Fleetwood Mac concert. During the concert, band member Lindsay Buckingham kept pointing up at Geoffrey and smiling and nodding. Buckingham went behind a huge speaker and peeked out at us like he was trying to play some weird game of hide-and-seek. No one sat next to us so it was obvious to us and others that Buckingham was singling us out from the other hundreds of people there. Other concertgoers turned and stared at us. Geoffrey had his arms up in the air and appeared to be in a trance during all of this. I was just as mystified as everyone else. There have been rumors for decades that Buckingham and bandmate Stevie Nicks are involved in occultic practices. I have no idea if it is true or not but something freaky happened at that concert.

PLAYING WITH FIRE

Geoffrey discovered that someone had allegedly been murdered or committed suicide in his house. We tried to find more information. Trips to the library and searches on the fledgling internet didn't reveal much. Geoffrey told me that he kept dreaming of seeing writing in blood on the walls of his house. We wanted to know more. We got the bright idea to try to talk to this spirit with a Oija board. I understand now how stupid this was…

I had only had one prior experience with a Oija board back in junior high school at a party as a gag. Some boy and I sat down with the thing and asked it something dumb like "Do demons drink beer?" The marker had slowly moved over to

79

say "No." I am positive that neither of us moved the marker. I could see his fingers barely touching the marker and I knew I wasn't moving it. That thing moved itself. We looked at each other, said "heck no." threw the game down and ran out of the room. I hadn't touched one since then.

According to my strict Southern Baptist upbringing, things like Oija Boards are dangerous and sinful. That is probably a wise stance. I don't know exactly how or why they work. But I believe that they do indeed work. At least that had been my experience. However I was throwing all the rest of my Baptist roots out the window then, so why not this one too?

So we bought one and sat down in Geoffrey's kitchen one evening to try it out. We turned out the lights and lit a candle to set the appropriate ghostly mood. I had a small spiral notepad and pen to write down anything it might say to us.

We lightly touched our fingertips to the marker and started with a simple question. "Are you here?"

We held our breath during the first few seconds as the marker sat motionless after our question. Then the marker twitched. It was a tiny motion, almost imperceptible. My heart jumped. Then it began to move shakily toward the top of the board. It accelerated as it moved as if whatever unseen phantom pushing it across the table was gaining courage. It stopped to rest directly over the YES.

Geoffrey and I paused for a moment, incredulous that it had actually worked. I scribbled down the question and answer into my notepad and placed my fingers back onto the marker.

Geoffrey asked another question, "Do you want to talk to us?"

The marker began moving almost immediately this time. It circled around and slid toward the middle of the board. Stopped. Twisted back around and moved up again to stop directly over the YES. I wrote this down.

We decided to ask a more complicated question. "What is your name?"

The marker deliberately moved from letter to letter to spell out the name MARK. … yikes.

I was horrified that this was working. I knew this was bad. Part of me wanted to throw the game across the room and run out of there. Another other part of me was eerily fascinated. How far could this go? How complicated of an answer could we get?

So then Goeffrey asked "What happened to you here?"

The marker started jerking around slightly for a few seconds and stopped. Then with one swift motion, the point whirled around and quickly lurched toward me, past the end of the board and off the edge of the table. It clattered onto the floor beside me. As it fell to the floor, a quick hard push shoved my shoulder, hard enough that it scooted my chair backwards away from the table. Geoffrey clearly hadn't touched me or my chair. Something else, something invisible and sinister had done this. I sat there in shock.

Immediately after this we heard a loud crash like breaking glass coming from the bedroom.

We were terrified. We stared at each other, afraid to move for a few moments.

Cautiously we got up, and turned on all the lights in the entire house, carefully avoiding the bedroom. Finally we dared to peek through the doorway. A glass lamp had been hurled across the room and landed on the floor. The power cord had been jerked from the wall and snaked straight out on the floor beside the lamp in the direction of the table where it had been sitting. We had both clearly heard the sound of shattering glass but the lamp was not broken. We searched but could find no other damage anywhere in the house. No broken glass anywhere.

Well that was enough for me. I was finished with that creepy Oija board for good. I demanded that we take it outside somewhere and burn it to ashes. So we did. We drove out into the country and burned the board, the box and pointer and my handwritten notes as well. I watched it all burn. I saw my notes on a piece of paper shrivel up into the flames. And that was that. I thought.

About a week later at Geoffrey's house, he opened a cabinet looking for something. I heard him say, "Oh no." He didn't want to show me what he had found. I insisted. And he opened the cabinet to show a Oija board game sitting in there.

Now this could have been another Oija board game. Geoffrey could have somehow rigged all of this up as a silly prank, I guess. When he opened the box, we stared in horror at a crumpled piece of notebook paper. There on that familiar piece of paper were my notes from the night we had played the game. My notes were sitting right there in that game box, my notes in my handwriting... my scratchy unmistakable handwriting. I had watched those same notes burn into a pile of ashes. How could this possibly be?

I had never experienced anything like this before. I had no idea that demons could manipulate matter. I had no idea they could bring things back after they had burned up. What couldn't they do? This refuted all the rules I thought I knew. The implications were ominous. I had to get away from this.

I never went to that house again. I was done with that house and done with Geoffrey. This was all just too much. I was playing with a dangerous fire and I needed to get out. We broke up soon afterwards.

DRUGGED

I was no longer suicidal but still severely depressed, continuing to take my psychiatrist prescribed mix of antidepressants, mood stabilizers, and sleeping pills. I was also drinking alcohol... a lot of alcohol... and that is a toxic combination.

I was a functional addict. During the day I held my job and even started my own website development business during this time (over twenty five years later, I am still running this very successful business). I found a cute little house to rent and moved out of my parent's house. I paid my bills. On the surface I seemed fine.

On evenings and weekends I became a completely different person. I had collected a group of friends at this point, drinking buddies. And I had met several other guys on internet dating sites but nothing serious. My weekends became a series of intoxicated inanities. I often drank until I blacked out. I started having *brownouts*, when I got drunk and acted crazy but later had no memory of it. I woke up in unfamiliar places and had no idea how I got there. My inner life was an insane jumble.

My psychiatrist diagnosed me as extremely bipolar and even psychotic because I confessed to her that I heard voices. She of course didn't believe in demons. To her all of my symptoms could be neatly explained and treated by modern secular psychiatry. The problem is that modern psychiatry practices don't work very well. Pills can't cure spiritual problems.

We tried a variety of drug combinations and then she put me on lithium. Lithium might have kept me alive, but it killed everything about me. I was a zombie in a thick drugged haze. People taking lithium are easy to spot with their blank expressions, glazed eyes, sallow skin and dull hair. That was me. Lithium is a wicked drug. It completely dissolved all of my emotions, not just the bad emotions but the good ones too. I wasn't depressed anymore so my doctor had accomplished her purpose. I didn't care about anything anymore. Nothing at all.

Thank goodness, for whatever reason, the extreme personality shift alarmed even my doctor. She took me off of the lithium after about six months. If she hadn't taken me off of it herself, I would have stayed on it forever. Lithium is a trap. I would never have tried to get better while I was taking it. I just didn't care.

I still kept taking various drug cocktails she prescribed. I kept drinking way too much alcohol. I never admitted to my doctor about the alcohol. That part wasn't her fault. The blackouts and brownouts and insane behavior continued.

This crazy double life lasted for three years. I was sleepwalking through life, drugged and drunk. My demon was ecstatic. She didn't need to scream at me anymore. She really didn't need to do anything anymore except bask in her victory.

She had defeated me. I was ruined. I belonged to her completely.

2001. NEW YEARS.

I've been changed
And I'll never be the same.
My soul's on fire
With a holy inspiration.

And I've seen things
That I never could explain.
My heart leaps up
At this glorious creation.

I've been given
Life again!

from "Morning"
song lyrics by Blue Tapp

Everything changed one winter night in 2001.

I was at a bar partying with friends getting wasted as usual.
We closed down the bar. I was way too drunk to be driving
home and the weather was terrible… snowing, freezing, icy. I
got behind the wheel anyway and drunkenly sped off into the
frozen night.

At some point along the route I skidded on ice, careened off the highway, and catapulted over a ditch into the grass. My car whirled around in circles, out of control. I smacked into a speed limit sign and it shot up and over my car. Finally my car skid to a stop. It was a black night and I could barely see anything outside of the car. I wasn't even sure where I was. I sat in my car for a few minutes stunned, thoughts tumbling in slow motion around in my drunken brain trying to figure out what to do. Fortunately one of my friends had been following me. He stopped on the shoulder when he saw my car fly off the road. He took me home where I slept off my hangover.

The next day was sunny and warmer and I got a ride out to my car to wait for the tow truck. When I got to my car I discovered what I hadn't been able to see in the darkness the previous night. My spinning car had stopped only yards away from a steep embankment that dropped sheerly down to the highway below the overpass. If I had skidded another few yards, my story would have ended very differently that night. The tow truck driver remarked that I was very lucky. A guy had gone off the road in that same spot the week before. He slid off the embankment and was killed.

He slid off that same embankment and he died…

That could have been me.

That should have been me.

In that moment I felt a rush of air and a deafening crash in my spirit. I distinctly heard a stern voice say, "This is your last chance. If you don't turn around I will never save you again."

The voice was so loud that at first I thought it had been audible. The tow truck driver apparently hadn't heard anything and kept talking to me. And so we continued our business of towing my car back to the road.

I was changed… forever.

I knew God had spoken to me. I believed what He had said. He was done bailing me out. No more angels would be sent to protect me from my own stupidity. My ninth life had been cashed in. I had to change or die.

So I changed.

SOBER

The first thing I did was to quit drinking alcohol. Cold turkey. I threw away every single drop and never touched it again for many years.

Next I set up a plan to slowly wean myself off of all the prescription drugs…anti-depressants, mood stabilizers and sleeping pills. I was too addicted to safely stop all at once. I had experienced running out of my sleeping pills before and the withdrawals were dreadful, cold shakes, panic attacks, the whole deal. My doctor had warned me that stopping the medication abruptly could be life threatening. So I worked up a plan to take smaller and smaller dosages until I would be completely clean of them by my 34th birthday, April 1, 2001.

And that is exactly what I did. By my birthday, I had been completely clean from prescription drugs for several weeks, and cold turkey clean from alcohol since the first week of January. I did it all without my psychiatrist. She wouldn't have approved of my plan. She told me I needed to be on medication for the rest of my life. So I never went to see her again. I never went to any sort of AA meetings or talked to any kind of counselor. It was just me and God. I don't necessarily recommend getting clean that way. In my case, God was the only counselor I needed.

HEALED

Today, over two decades later, I am completely healed.

God has healed me of my drug addiction. I have been drug free ever since that winter in 2001.

God also delivered me from my demon again. There was no slamming door this time. After that day with the tow truck, she quietly slunk out of my mind and never returned. And now I've learned how to keep her gone for good.

Here's perhaps the biggest victory…

I am totally healed from depression.

I have never struggled with depression for over two decades now. I've gone through some hard times since then, some really difficult times. I've felt sadness and anger at times. Those are temporary emotions so very different from soul-killing depression. I have learned how to be healed from depression. When the blackness of depression creeps anywhere close to me, I now know how to fight it and win… really win… not just push it down, put on a happy face and act like everything is okay. I've learned how to actually be profoundly happy, content and at peace deep my soul. Yes it is really true. I'm not faking it. I am healed.

I believe that everyone is capable of being healed from depression as well. I will tell you my secrets…

TIME

The healing process wasn't painless. My immune system was weakened as I gradually weaned myself off the drugs and I got very sick. It was a frigid winter and I spent most of it alone at home dog sick…sore throat, fever, shakes. I ran my website development business full time from my home now and didn't need to go anywhere. So I stayed at home alone in my house for months.

That's exactly what I needed — time. Time to heal and get strong. Time to learn *how* to get well. Time to learn how to *stay* well.

COMING BACK TO JESUS

I dove into God. I began reading the Bible again and praying. I read a great book about God's love for us, *The Sacred Romance,*[9] and rekindled my love affair with Jesus.

God took me to the *school of the spirit* during those months. Just Jesus and me. I wasn't going to church. I didn't talk to anyone except God. No one helped or guided me through this time. I prayed and read the Bible and God met me there. It was raw Holy Spirit. It was deeply authentically real.

Over those next months, God showed me step by step how to heal from my depression. God taught me how to control my thoughts - to recognize and reject the negative thoughts that

---

[9] Curtis, Brent and John Eldredge. *The Sacred Romance: Drawing Closer to the Heart of God.* Nashville: Thomas Nelson, 1997. Print.

fed depression. I learned to repeat this mantra to myself constantly about every single thought...

Does this thought benefit my soul?

If the answer was NO, I immediately dropped that thought. Immediately. No sitting around thinking about it for even a few minutes. I learned how to stop all non-beneficial thoughts *immediately.*

This was the huge key to my healing... taking control of my thought life. Our culture does not teach us how to do this or even that it can be done. Our culture tells us instead to indulge our whims and emotions. Most people are completely at the mercy of their own emotions. Our emotions are fickle and cannot be trusted. Emotions are unstable and can swing drastically from moment to moment. A life based on emotion is a life built on shifting sands. Stable happiness and real healing is not possible in a life built on emotions. The next unhappy situation or hardship will cause it all to come crashing down.

All of this takes place in the mind... in our thoughts... in the thought chatter that fills up our minds every minute of every day. Our thought life can be either life or death to our souls. We can and *must* control our thoughts if we want to be truly emotionally and spiritually healthy.

This became my mantra... *Does this thought benefit my soul?*

Minute by minute I consciously examined each thought and asked myself this question over and over and over, a thousand times a day if necessary - does this thought benefit my soul?

I had to learn how to observe my thoughts, to rise up out of my mental soup of emotions and take the reins of what was happening in my brain.

Does this thought benefit my soul?

Notice what I *wasn't* asking. I wasn't asking if it was a happy thought. I wasn't asking if it was a pleasant thought. I was asking if each thought *benefitted my soul*.

Happy pleasant thoughts were great. Thoughts that did benefit my soul also included lots of hard things I needed to work through to continue healing… forgiving myself for all my stupid mistakes… forgiving others for hurting me… learning to trust God instead of myself… learning to accept my life situation as it was with grace and peace.

Thoughts that did not benefit my soul included negative judgmental thoughts about myself or others. No more nursing old wounds that I gave myself or were inflicted upon me by others. I used to spend a lot of time reliving painful memories and wallowing in my hurt. I played hours of mental what if movies… what if I had done this instead? What if that had happened instead? I fantasized about things I wished I had done or said differently. All these thoughts had to go. The past is the past and it can't be changed. There is no benefit in reliving each negative memory over and over and over again like a broken record.

I learned the healing process of *remembering, forgiving and dismissing*. I had to learn how to really dismiss and let go of *all* the hurt and unforgiveness. Nothing that hindered my healing process could remain. Nothing could stay hidden in a corner somewhere. It all had to be sifted through methodically, thought by thought by thought.

I also used to spend a lot of time fantasizing about things I wanted to happen in the future... a fantasy romance, dream job, getting a lot of money, becoming famous. Many people spend a lot of time fantasizing about all the things they want... things that we think would make us happy if we could only get this relationship, that job or that thing. Spending all that time focusing on what I didn't have was a huge source of my unhappiness. So yep, it all had to go too.

I learned how to live in the moment, how to really be present and enjoy each moment. I learned how to accept my life situation exactly as it was with peace and gratitude. I learned how to be thankful.

It was hard work. But it worked. It still works. It was so very worthwhile.

THE FIRST VISION

Soon after my self imposed exile, I experienced my very first vision.

I was in the shower one morning when it happened. I always prayed in the mornings while I was showering.

A doorway in my soul blasted open and my spirit was taken to heaven. I was immediately transported there through no effort of my own. I hadn't begun meditating back then and wasn't practicing stilling my thoughts yet. I was just praying, good old normal spoken and thought prayer. God just took me there. No warning. Nothing. Just instant crazy intense vision. It was quite a shock.

In my vision, I was taken to the holy place that is so familiar to me now. Back then I had no idea what was happening or where I was.

In my vision, my spirit floated above a sea of millions of people. A blinding golden light was suspended above the multitudes of people. I somehow understood that this blinding light was the glory of God. The light was so brilliant and powerful that it was excruciatingly painful. It pushed into my being with intense pressure. It felt as if every cell in my body were going to burst.

I slowly descended down into the throng of humanity. Everyone stared upward fixated on the fantastic golden light, the glory of God. Each person was either in abject ecstacy or absolute horror at what they were seeing. They shook uncontrollably and screamed "I had no idea! I had no idea! I had no idea!"

I felt in my spirit that this was the end of the world when millions of humans are at once simultaneously face to face with God. This was that moment each person realized the undeniable power of the Creator, that moment when they understand completely their own small frail existence. I had never witnessed such combined passion and terror. Their screams pierced into the center of my soul. I felt terrible dread but also the most intense euphoria. This place, radiant with the brilliant glory of God, was the most exquisitely beautiful place I had ever seen.

My body floated back up out of their midst again. The profound love of God emanated out of the golden flaming orb and surrounded me. It was terribly painful but so magnificent that I never wanted it to end.

In the sky behind the golden light I saw a woman who I assumed to be Mother Mary wearing a dazzling blue robe and glorious shining halo. God's voice said to me, "She will help you." *(I was quite confused about this apparent vision of Mary at the time. God has since explained this to me along with more amazing miracles that will be the subject of a future book.)*

The vision abruptly ended and I was back in my shower lying on the floor of the tub. Sunlight filtering through my bathroom window was dull and dark after the brilliant light in my vision. During the vision I had apparently fallen in the tub but I had no memory of it. I had been completely unaware of my physical body during the vision. Later I would notice a large bruise on my leg which must have happened when I fell.

I sat there in the shower for a long while, letting the warm water wash over me, thoughts racing wildly as I tried to understand what had just happened. I had never experienced anything remotely like this before. My body still hurt. I would be sore for several days.

The vision seemed so real. I thought my face must be glowing with light as had the face of Moses after his encounters with God on Mount Sinai. I had seen God's glory!

I climbed out of the shower and looked in the mirror, and I only saw my unchanged face staring back at me.

Internally I was radically changed. I had seen heaven. I had experienced the glory of God and lived....

Right after the vision, I assumed that I had entered a new phase with God. I smugly thought I would have these visions all the time now.

It would be 16 years before I would have such another intense vision.

God is always in control of this. God determines if and when and what... always.

So I continued on, seeking God as best I could. I found a good non-denominational church and got involved. I kept building my business.

I met my future husband, who moved into the house next door. We met when he came over to tell me (nicely) that my tree was hitting his roof. He admitted to me later that he had seen me working in my yard and the tree story was a ruse to meet me.

I had been praying for God to bring the right mate for me and God moved him right next door. My husband is an amazing man who had also been saved from a traumatic life full of bad decisions, just like me. We knew immediately that God had connected us. We got married after a quick engagement and have enjoyed a fantastic marriage and deep friendship for over twenty years now.

The two of us helped a small group of people start a new church that we attended for seven years. We went on several mission trips to Belize and witnessed God do many powerful things. God continues to work powerfully in our lives and has recently moved us across our state to set up a homestead ministry in rural Missouri while we wait for His next instructions.

God blessed our wonderful marriage and friendship. My husband has four fabulous grown children who I love dearly. God has blessed my website business and over two and a half decades after beginning the business, it continues to provide well and I still love it. Our lives are full and rich beyond anything I could ever have imagined, beyond anything I might deserve. Words don't exist that are strong enough to convey how thankful I am to God for the floods of grace and mercy I have been given.

PART 3. HEALING FROM DEPRESSION

A NOTE FROM THE AUTHOR: PART 3 IS DIFFERENT!

Part 3 of this book deviates from my story to dig into some deeper issues. It begins by speaking directly to those who struggle with depression and guides readers through the process I followed to healing. I also explore how relationship to God and Jesus connect to my continued wellbeing and what it means to be saved. This section delves pretty deeply into some theological ideas and that may or may not be everyone's cup of tea. Some readers love this stuff. Others prefer to stick to the story. I feel the message of this section needed to be included in this book. But Part 3 may be skipped without missing any of the storyline. Part 4 returns to my visions.

~ Blue

MY HEALING.

I lost my life
But I got it back again.
From a stale cold grave
To sweet illumination.

Into the sun
From the snow and the rain,
I travel home
With a peaceful expectation.
I've been given
Life again.

from "Morning"
song lyrics by Blue Tapp

The truth is that God healed me from my depression. Only God is our ultimate healer. Only through the blood of Jesus Christ are we united with God, filled with the Holy Spirit and made whole. Only through Jesus Christ can we attain true lasting peace and joy in this life.

However my healing from depression was not instantaneous. God is certainly capable of instantly healing people from any illness if He chooses to do so. And sometimes He does!

God often instead chooses to *partner with us* to reach our healing. God accomplishes the divine healing work as we surrender to Him and follow His guidance. He sometimes will lead us through a series of steps, a pathway to reach and remain in that place of healing. Many times that pathway, those steps we take, are actually an integral part of the healing itself. Whatever those steps are, whatever He teaches us along the way, are the skills that we need to be healed and continue to live out our healing. This is our training, learning how to "run with perseverance the race marked out for us."[10]

This is what God did for me. He *taught* me how not to be depressed.

Then He told me to tell others about it which is what you are reading right now. I believe He may want to take others through a similar path of healing and maybe reading this book is part of that process for someone out there.

Maybe it is why YOU are reading this book right now.

If so, please know that I have been praying for YOU. I will continue to pray for you, that God will use these words in this book to help heal you. I pray for you to know the depth and

---

[10] *Hebrews 12:1 (NIV)*

104

riches of God's amazing love for you. I pray for you to be healed, whole, full of the peace and joy of Jesus Christ.

Here is how God healed me from depression...

THE PURPOSE OF PAIN

My former psychiatrist would be astonished to see how happy and healthy I am today. I didn't bother going to see her again after I decided to get off the prescribed drugs. She wouldn't have approved of my plan to stop taking them. She told me I needed to take drugs for the rest of my life.

She was wrong.

I liked my psychiatrist. She was a nice lady. But she was essentially a legal drug pusher. I talked to her for 30 minutes every month and she gave me drugs. She never tried to guide me through the internal work I needed to do to actually get well. She wasn't an evil person. She was just following her training.

She was wrong.

So many of us who are trying to find happiness in prescription bottles, do not *need* to be drugged. For many people, pills are a bandaid on their problems and they never really get well.

They absolve themselves from doing the hard mental, emotional, and spiritual work required to really heal because they have their prescription, their doctor's permission slip, allowing them to skip the work. They think pills are the cure. They aren't. Drugs cannot *cure* depression.

Please understand, I believe there are *some* people who *should* be on medication to protect themselves or others. I don't think permanent drug use is ever ideal. But this is a fallen world full of fallen people and will never be ideal. Sometimes permanent medication is just the least harmful option. However I think these cases comprise only the tiniest percentage of our grossly overdrugged society.

I also believe there may be times when prescription drugs can be helpful *temporarily*. There is a helpful place for prescription drugs. We would be so much better off if the drugs were only considered to be a *temporary* aid until the patient is strong enough to start doing the actual work of healing on their own.

This is not what I see happening. Many psychiatrists, like mine, train their patients to believe that the drugs *are* the cure instead of guiding them through the difficult process of actually getting better. Perhaps many psychiatrists really do *believe* that drugs *can* cure depression. Others are just playing along for profit. Regardless of whether psychiatrists are knowingly lying or really believe in the message they peddle, the message they (and the pharmaceutical industries) are preaching is not true.

Drugs cannot cure depression.

Antidepressants *can* make you *feel* better temporarily. So why not just take them and feel better? Because it's not real healing. Antidepressants mask the bad feelings that are telling you something is wrong and needs to be dealt with. Hiding those emotions with drugs only guarantees that the patient will never address their actual problems.

Pain can be beneficial. I know it's not the happiest message, but sometimes we need to feel pain in order to get better. Pain can be the catylist we need to get off the couch and do the work needed to address the pain.

Masking emotional pain with drugs is like taking painkillers to numb an infected wound. You might feel better temporarily but unless the infection is addressed and removed, the patient is not going to really get better. In fact, if that infected wound isn't treated properly, the patient might end up losing a limb or worse.

Emotional pain works in a similar way. It tells us that there is something wrong inside that needs some work. Pain guides us to the problem area so we know where the work needs to be done.

DO YOU WANT TO BE HEALED?

I believe that almost everyone is capable of doing the same mental/emotional/spiritual work God led me through to get healing… I'm not talking about just a temporary feel good from a bottle… but real deep lasting authentic healing.

Do you want that?

You can get it.

You've got to work for it.

It is so worth it.

It takes time and it isn't easy. But it works. And if you do the work I believe you will receive healing.

Here's the most important thing to understand as you begin…

Healing from depression starts in *your mind.*

The war for your soul, for your peace and victory, takes place in your mind. So that is where the battle for healing must begin.

My first step to healing was to take control of my thoughts and emotions. Our culture doesn't teach us how to do this. Our culture doesn't even acknowledge that it is possible. Our culture tells us to worship our feelings and that we should be the center of our own universe. Both of these ideas lead directly to depression and misery.

In the Bible, Paul encourages us to "demolish arguments and every proud thing that is raised up against the knowledge of Christ and we take every thought captive to obey Christ."[11] This is what I'm talking about, taking "every thought captive." How do we do this?

FEELINGS & THOUGHTS

Have you ever been angry or hurt and then gotten over it? Have you ever had good or bad feelings about someone and realized later that you were wrong?

Feelings can shift on a whim. They change over time. Feelings are irrational unreliable sentiments. They cannot be trusted. Feelings alone most certainly should not be used to make important decisions. That is exactly how many people make their decisions, based only on their feelings. Many people are enslaved by their emotions. When the bad feelings come, they are helpless to defend themselves against them. And so they wallow in sadness, anger, and depression.

---

[11] *2 Corinthians 10:5 (CSB)*

It doesn't have to be this way.

Once you see feelings and emotions for what they are, you can choose to enjoy the pleasant ones and disregard the negative ones. You may not be able to keep from *feeling* the bad emotions. You can be in *control* of how your feelings affect you. You can control how you choose to respond to your feelings. *You* can be in control of your emotions rather than being controlled by them.

Your emotions play themselves out in your thoughts. So inside your mind is the ground where this battle must be waged, by learning to observe and control your thoughts.

Emotion driven thoughts are just one of the many different kinds of thoughts clamoring around in our brains. The overall battle will eventually need to address much more than solely emotion driven thoughts. It's a good place to start because emotion driven thoughts are usually the most powerful, especially for many women. Emotion driven thoughts often do the most damage. They can be like a blindfolded swordsman randomly slashing your soul to pieces. Don't let this fickle pillager ravage your life.

You have to *train your mind.*

As I was overcoming depression, God taught me the mantra "Is this good for my soul?" I asked myself this question about *every* thought.

"Is this thought good for my soul?"

I had to be extremely intentional about my thought life. I had to examine every single thought as it flashed through my brain. It was hard work, used a lot of brain power. It was mentally exhausting. Sometimes I messed up and forgot to do it. But I just started back up. I kept practicing this mantra about every thought, over and over.

Every. Single. Thought…

"Is this thought good for my soul?"

If the answer was no, then I immediately stopped thinking that thought.

Immediately.

No wallowing in self pity for a few minutes. No revisiting how someone said something that hurt my feelings. No fantasizing about that spiteful comeback I wish I had said to someone. If the thought wasn't good for my soul then I dropped it *immediately*.

This wasn't easy to do. It took a lot of practice to train my mind to work this way. It was easy to slip back into old thought patterns. When that happened, I did not spend a moment berating myself for failure (which would not have been good for my soul!); I just got back to it.

It was so worth the work. It worked. After many months of this, it became my habitual way of thinking and eventually completely rewired my brain for happiness rather than depression.

There is a huge spiritual component to this as well. Demons are real and most of us are affected by them whether we realize it or not. I've seen them and experienced their influence. They can and will destroy our lives if we let them. I believe that so much depression is actually a spiritual condition induced by demonic oppression.

On the other hand, God and His angelic forces are also very real and much more powerful than any demon. Believers in Christ are filled with His Holy Spirit and given authority over demons if we will only learn how to use it. Learning and practicing spiritual warfare can be very helpful in combatting these evil forces.

A library of books are needed to fully explore the subject of spiritual warfare and there are a lot of good ones out there. But the most basic fact to know is that our power rests in the Name of Jesus. If you are a Christian, then you are covered by the Name of Jesus and you have the right to invoke His Name to battle against evil spirits.

As I was training my mind, I would often suspect that demonic forces were attacking my thoughts, trying to drag me back down into depression. Any time that happened, I spoke outloud, "In the Name of Jesus, I command you, demon, to be quiet and get out of here!" Every time I did that I would feel immediate relief. They might come back to bother me again later. But we can invoke the Name of Jesus as many times as needed. There is no limit. There is great power in the Name of Jesus. Demons must flee at His Name.

OUR IDENTITY

Our thoughts are not who we are. Many people equate their identity with their mind… with their thoughts. I did for most of my life.

Let me say that again…

Our identity is not our thoughts.

Our thoughts actually form a false identity, our ego, that we portray to the world and even to ourselves. The internal chatter that fills our minds is a very surface level part of us. It is not actually who we are, our deepest essence, our true identity.

Deep down within each one of us there is an eternal part of us that is actually our true identity. It is not our thoughts. It is deeper than the words and language that form our thoughts. The Bible refers to this eternal part of us often. Jesus calls it our *"soul"*[12] or our *"psychē"*[13] in the Greek. Paul calls it our *"inner being."*[14] This is the part of us that will still exist after we die and our bodies and brains return to dust.

Our emotions and thoughts are mortal; some day they will just stop. Our souls are eternal. They will exist forever. Our soul is the part of us that God is drawing to Himself. Our soul is the part of us that either seeks to commune with our Creator or reject Him. Our souls are our true eternal identities. They are infinitely more important and valuable than the rest of us. Becoming more aware of your soul, your true identity, is the most important element of healing. If you want your healing to be deep, lasting, and real, then it must reach down into your soul.

SOULS

It is possible, and quite common, for people to be completely unaware of the existence of their own soul. Some ancient cultures were more aware of their souls. Our modern western culture has lost touch with our true identities. We have shifted our focus from our eternal selves to surface pleasures and physical ambitions. We have become so separated from our

---

[12] *Matthew 10:28 (NIV)*

[13] *Strongs Concordance G5590*

[14] *Ephesians 3:16 (NIV)*

114

true selves that many people don't even believe that we *have* a soul. We have replaced an eternal God with temporary rotting idols. Deep inside we cannot help but know, if only subconsciously, that everything we desire is fleeting and temporary. Every part of us, our bodies and thoughts, is going to die and end, *except* our eternal souls. Shouldn't our focus then be on our souls, the one thing that will remain?

How do you become more aware your soul? How do you tap into it?

Here's a simple exercise to *begin*. Hold your hand in front of you. Then close your eyes. How do you *know* your hand is there? You should be able to feel a tingling sensation in your hand verifying that it is there. Focus on that feeling. You can move that tingling feeling up and down your body. This is the most basic interaction between your mind and your soul. Learning to quiet your mind through meditation allows you to further this interaction with your soul. You can train yourself to separate your true identity, your soul, from your thoughts and become an observer of your thoughts rather than being trapped inside of them.

Many Christians are scared of meditation. The word evokes images of orange robed monks praying to Buddha, new age paganism, Indian yogis teaching prayer positions to demonic deities… yep, those are all real things. And yes many people do use meditation as part of pagan, decidedly non-Christian practices.

However meditation itself is not the problem. Meditation is merely continued or extended thought; contemplation; spiritual introspection.[15] To meditate simply means to exercise control over our thoughts. What meditation is used for determines if it is a good or bad practice.

That is why I call it "meditative prayer," to differentiate it from non-Christian pagan uses. I use meditation as a form of prayer to grow closer to Jesus Christ. Practicing meditative prayer allows me to "be still"[16] and rest in God's presence. Through meditative prayer, God has taught me to quiet my thoughts and focus on my soul, my true eternal self, and commune with Him. As a believer in Jesus Christ, I am filled with God's Holy Spirit. God resides there, in my soul. By focusing on my soul, where the Holy Spirit resides, I am able to be more fully aware and present with God's Holy Spirit. This process can be very healing.

MEDITATIVE PRAYER

I've briefly described my meditation process earlier in this book. But here it is in more detail.

---

[15] *From the Collins English Dictionary - Complete & Unabridged 2012 Digital Edition*

[16] *Psalm 46:10*

I begin by sitting in a comfortable place alone. It is important to feel comfortable, unwatched, and completely free from self-consciousness. I start with several deep breaths. Sit up straight with legs up and crossed or both feet on the floor, shoes off if possible. I hold my arms to my sides and palms pressed together against my chest in prayer position or facing upwards in a posture to receive from God.

(If you are a Christian concerned about possible demonic interference while your mind has been stilled, start with a spiritual warfare prayer of protection. "In the Name of Jesus, I rebuke, revoke, and renounce any and all demonic connections to me and command all demons to be quiet and get out of this place. I am bought with the blood of Jesus Christ, sealed and filled with the Holy Spirit. I am a child of the King and I put on the Holy, spotless, sanctified, pure perfection of Christ through the blood of Jesus. Come, Holy Spirit, fill me, surround me, completely saturate this place. Lord Jesus, surround me with Your angels in a hedge of protection against any demonic plans or assignments. Thank You, Jesus!")

I first slowly look around and really *see* my surroundings — quieting down my thought chatter and only observing my surroundings without making any mental judgments about what I'm looking at… the walls, furniture, floor, ceiling, grass, flowers and sky. I'm not thinking about the past or future, but only observing *now*. God's glorious Creation is "perfect in beauty" from which "God shines forth."[17]

---

[17] *Psalm 50:2 (NIV)*

Then I close my eyes and observe all the sounds I hear —
delving into the layers of sounds until I'm aware of every
sound… birds singing, cars and planes going by, dogs barking,
the hum of the air conditioner. My soul drinks deeply the
majestic song of God's works; it is "a hymn of praise to our
God."[18]

I often then cover my ears with my hands and listen to the
sound of my breathing. I observe all the functions of my body
that are taking place right *now* — my breaths going in and out,
my heart beating, the blood moving through my veins; I am
aware of my muscles, bones, and organs. "I am fearfully and
wonderfully made; [God's] works are wonderful."[19]

I become aware of the life inside of me, my soul. It is the
eternal part of me, where God's Holy Spirit resides — not my
thoughts but my consciousness. I can feel it tingling in my
hands and my chest and then up and down my body. I take
deep breaths and focus on this enjoyable feeling.

At this point my thoughts have usually become very quiet and
my breathing has slowed way down. The more I practice this
the easier it becomes to enter into this peaceful state. If an
unwanted thought invades my brain, I visualize myself putting
that thought into a box, closing the box, and setting it firmly on

---

[18] *Psalm 40:3 (NIV)*

[19] *Psalm 139:14 (NIV)*

a shelf. Then I return to my quiet. This meditation process is part of my daily prayer time and often if my mind wanders, I will whisper the words of St. Teresa de Avila, "Let nothing disturb the silence of this moment with you, my Lord."

I meditate like this for at least 30 minutes a day. I used to set my phone alarm when I began and used a soothing chime sound for the alarm. This way I don't have to worry about time or keep checking my watch. I just relax into the meditation until I hear the alarm. Often I don't feel finished when my 30 minute chime rings and keep on meditating as long as I feel is needed. Today I no longer use an alarm. I've learned how to stay in a meditative state much longer now and my meditations usually last 90 minutes or longer. But 30 minutes is a good goal. If 30 minutes seems too hard, start with a shorter time (even five minutes is better than none) and slowly increase over time.

Practicing 30 minutes of this meditative prayer every day will change your life. You will learn how to control your thoughts and not be at the mercy of your emotions. You will begin to feel more peace, satisfaction and joy. I believe that this practice can be helpful for Christians and non-Christians alike. But for those of us filled with the Holy Spirit, God can also use this time to communicate with you. You may never experience visions like I have (or you might!) but you *will* experience God's presence in some way if you desire it. Emptying your mind of your thoughts regularly creates a space where God can work with you. If you *want* to make space for God, then God *will* meet you there some how, some way. I don't know exactly what that will look like in your life. I promise it *will* happen.

LIFE IS HARD

Let's get back to the surface for a moment...

Let's face it, this is a hard world and life is full of pain.

That is just the *truth*.

Everyone experiences pain and hurt and sickness no matter how rich or how smart they are. Things are going to be unfair. You aren't going to always get your way.

That is just the *truth*.

Trying to deny this truth is only a bandaid on a bloody stump. You can get away with it during good times. Some day, some how, life is going to get difficult and that false tower of denial is going to come crashing down. We're much better off confronting this truth and dealing with it now instead of from the underside of a tragedy.

Repeat after me: *life is hard and full of pain.*

How you *respond* to this truth will determine if you are a happy or depressed person. Becoming a happy person doesn't mean that you learn how to avoid difficulties or pain. That is impossible. You cannot be healed from depression if you require your life to be easy or painfree.

The key to your happiness or lack of it really doesn't have much to do with the outward circumstances of your life at all. Your happiness is determined by *how* you *think* about the circumstances of your life. And you can control that.

First you have to understand and accept that pain and difficulty *are* going to happen to you. Trying to fight this truth is pointless. You can't win this fight and it will only fill you with despair. I'm not suggesting a pessimistic, fatalistic attitude. You can passionately work hard to improve your life and still accept that your life will inevitably include difficulties.

This doesn't mean that you *want* to have hardships. Nobody wants that. You *know* they will happen sooner or later. So when the hard times come, you don't feel that your life is over. You only have to bear the difficulties for a season. Accept them. Learn from them. There is much to be gained from our hardships. They make us stronger and wiser. The good times *will* eventually come again too. And when they do, you will have a deeper, more profound thankfulness for them than you ever had before the troubles began.

We must acknowledge that we aren't in control of the world. Plan as we might, we aren't even in control of our own lives.

There are bigger forces at play in this universe, much bigger than ourselves. In the grand scheme of the cosmos, we are actually quite small and powerless. Many of us like to believe we are in control of things; we spend a lot of time, money and effort attempting to fashion our lives. All it takes is a car crash, an unfortunate act of nature, a cancer diagnosis, or some other such disaster to reveal the truth of it. We are not afterall the master of our universe.

We are totally free to *think* the world revolves around us, of course. Most people do believe this. People who are the center of their own universe are the most wretched beings alive. No matter how they may act on the outside, they are always miserable.

Understanding your true place in this universe requires humility. Our culture doesn't teach humility. The more you worship yourself, the more of an unhappy selfish monster you will become. It is an interesting catch 22 situation. The harder you push and tug at life to get what you think you *deserve*, the more unhappy you will be. You will never be satisfied and people won't like to be around you.

As you shift your focus away from your physical and emotional self, you are no longer obsessed with meeting your own needs. As you practice focusing on your eternal soul and on God, your life perspective inevitably begins to change. You are no longer offended when someone says or does something you don't like because you realize how insignificant it is. Your difficulties no longer feel insurmountable. You have more patience and are slower to anger. You begin to see that most things that may have bothered you before really don't matter very much. Learning to control your thoughts will give you a stable emotional/spiritual foundation on which you can exist.

Sometimes, in order to continue your healing from depression, you'll need to emotionally and spiritually work through past wounds. Some of us have been horribly abused and some of these deep hurts can take years, decades, to work through. I must tell you that some wounds will never completely go away in this life. You can learn to embrace them in forgiveness so that you can live with deep fulfillment and joy *along with* the wounds.

Woundedness doesn't equal defeat.

Woundedness can be turned into great strength and compassion. For your own sake you must be willing to release your unforgiveness or desires for vengeance. The person who wounded you is not hurt by your unforgiveness but *you* are. Leave revenge to God and seek the healing balm that is forgiveness.

In order to be healed from depression you must give up whatever injustices you feel you have a right to be angry about.

You must give up whatever injustices you feel you have a right to be sad about or to feel sorry for yourself about.

You must give up whatever injustices you are holding against anyone else.

You must give up your *right* to revenge.

Are you ready to do that?

FINDING GOD.

Our thoughts are real, they have power. Learning to control your thoughts can either open the doorway to God in your life or completely shut God out. The more you focus your thoughts on God, the more healing you will receive from depression. My relationship with God has been my strength and my victory. God has called me, instructed me, and walked with me to my healing every step of this journey. God is our Creator and Father. Only He is our ultimate healer.

I believe deeply in the existence of a personal God. I have always believed this. I know some people struggle to believe that God is real. I personally cannot understand that struggle. God's existence has always seemed so obvious to me when I consider the profound intricacy of the universe.

However, if you don't believe in God, or want to believe in God but cannot, I have a challenge for you. During your time of quiet meditation, in your spirit send out a question to God. Ask Him to reveal Himself to you. Don't put any stipulations on it. Don't ask for anything like money or success or some other physical gift. This isn't about *you* and God isn't some sort of lottery ticket. Just ask for relationship. *God if you're there, please show me.* If you mean it and you persist, God will respond to you some how, some way. I can't tell you exactly how He will respond to you. He will, I promise. Try it. Really, what do you have to lose?

Unbelief will make you blind to God's existence. The unbelieving will always find some way to explain away God's miracles. Athiests cannot perceive the wonderful works and presence of God. Believing in God is so beneficial to our own spiritual and mental wellbeing. When we fail to recognize the wonderful mysteries of God that are constantly all around us, we condemn ourselves to exist only in this temporary physical world. Believing that this cursed world is all there is can never be a very happy fulfilling existence. How could it be? This world really stinks sometimes!

Our postmodern culture conditions us to assume the negative about everything, that life is generally bad. So many people interpret everything unfavorably and believe that the world is indeed a terrible place. If we turn that around and assume the world is generally positive, and we are loved by a good God... everything changes. We begin to see connections and purpose where other people perceive only negative emptiness. By choosing to believe in the good, and in a loving good God, our eyes are opened to the good, and our world becomes good, filled with magic and beauty. Understanding this is a key to happiness.

IS GOD SPEAKING TODAY?

I believe that God indeed does choose sometimes to speak to us today in visions and messages. I didn't always believe this.

I was taught to mistrust anything mystical - that anything unexplainable is dangerous… that God said everything there is to say in the Bible and there is no more for Him to say. That belief seems terribly incomplete to me now.

Please know I am not implying that the Bible isn't true or extremely important. I believe strongly that the Bible is both true and of utmost importance. The Bible is God's personal letter to us, His instruction manual for us to understand who He is. It is our foundation for what is true. If we want to draw near to God, we must begin with the Bible.

I believe that God, the Creator of the Universe, is not *confined* to the Bible. He gave us His Word to learn about Him. The Bible comes first. It is our primary authority and everything should be tested against Scripture. And we have to be familiar with the Bible to do that. The more we delve into the Bible, the more we will learn about God's character and how He operates. He will not say or do anything that conflicts with the Word He has already given us.

God is still working. God is still very active and present in our lives today. He is still speaking to us. This gives me great joy and hope.

The Creator of the Universe is way more complex than we could ever fathom. How futile it is to think we mere humans could ever understand and explain everything completely. God is simply beyond our human comprehension. We can't possibly explain or understand the one who is big enough to create the universe out of nothing. Our brains are too feeble to ever fully comprehend something so immensely great and powerful as God.

If we could completely figure out God, then why would we even need Him? The quest to thoroughly understand and explain truth is an insult to God's greatness. It is our attempt to control our own destiny, which of course we cannot do. It is our vain attempt to contain God. God cannot be contained. Anything we grasp about God is only because He allows us to learn and has opened up our minds to perceive it. God is always the initiator. God is always absolutely in control.

I don't find this threatening. I find it comforting to be loved and known by such a fantastically big God who cannot be completely figured out. I love the mystery. I find it intriguing. I've observed that some Christian circles seem to feel threatened by mystery. They have a great fear of the unknown. I believe there is a spirit of fearfulness and legalism in many churches that blocks God from working there. This is why many Christian churches today feel dead and cold. This is why droves of young people have fled from organized Christianity.

GOD'S WORD

I do believe that the Bible is the true Word of God, the most important book that has ever existed in human history. It teaches us about God and how God works. I have read the Bible cover to cover many times, and continue to read through it every year. I study it daily. Every time I read through the Bible, I am profoundly changed for the better in some way. It is a beautiful, magical book full of great truth. It cannot be replaced by anything else as the foundation of the Christian faith.

It is so important to be familiar with the Bible to understand how God works and how He has worked throughout history. Knowledge of the Bible helps us to help discern messages that we think might be coming to us from God. If the message is obviously contradictory to truths we find in Scripture, then we'd better do some deeper digging and seeking.

It is certainly possible to think God is speaking to us when He isn't. We should always test the messages we think we are receiving. We are fallen humans afterall. We get a lot of things wrong. Comparing the message against Bible texts is the obvious first thing to check.

Believing that God gives messages and visions today is risky. It requires human beings to interpret experiences and that can be messy; emotions and imaginations can get in the way. We can and do get things wrong. This is why many churches dismiss the prophetic world today. They are missing out on such a fantastic powerful part of the Christian faith. They completely disregard the power of the Holy Spirit and His desire to interact with us. That, to me, is *much* riskier than believing God speaks to us today!

Really following and seeking God will always include some risk. Trying to completely sanitize everything and devise formulas to keep everyone from ever making mistakes is what the Pharisees in the Bible tried to do. They built up a complicated system of laws around the laws God gave them through Moses in the Old Testament. Israelites who tried to obey all of the Pharisaic laws would never even get close to disobeying one of God's laws. All legalistic religion is the same as this… a wall of rules to control us and keep us from making mistakes. Trying to live within a system of rules is a fearful joyless life. A system of rules cannot replace dynamic living relationship with God. God sent his son, Jesus, to earth in order to save us from a system of cold rules. Let's not put ourselves back under the futile legalistic chains that Jesus saved us from.

Fearful legalistic living can never bring about a victorious joyful freedom-filled life. Legalism can never draw you closer to God. It will never heal you from depression or make you spiritually whole. Jesus railed against the Pharisees over and over again. They are the only people, besides the temple moneychangers, He ever treated rudely. He called them "hypocrites" and told them they were "like whitewashed tombs, which look beautiful on the outside but on the inside are full of the bones of the dead and everything unclean. In the same way," He told them, "on the outside you appear to people as righteous but on the inside you are full of hypocrisy and wickedness."[20] That is how

---

[20] *Matthew 23: 27-28 NIV*

Jesus described legalism. When the Galatians were falling back into all the legalistic Jewish practices, Paul encouraged them that "it is for freedom that Christ has set us free. Stand firm, then, and do not let yourselves be burdened again by a yoke of slavery."[21] Paul describes legalism as *slavery*.

Freedom is the opposite of legalism. Freedom is seeking God without fear of breaking rules. Freedom is believing that if you try to draw near to God, He will guide you. Freedom is not being afraid of making mistakes because God is bigger and stronger than our mistakes. Faithfully seeking God without fear opens up the doorway to God's messages to us today. Faithfully seeking God without fear creates space in our lives where God can do what He wants to do with us, whatever that might be. Living a life of freedom includes freedom from the avoidable pit of depression. And "if the Son sets you free, you will be free indeed."[22]

We will explore the dangers of legalism a bit more in a bit but first…

---

[21] *Galatians 5:1 NIV*

[22] *John 8:36 (NIV)*

ARE YOU 'SAVED'?

This book would not be complete without a discussion about salvation, what it means to be 'saved,' and how to go about getting there. I hope that everyone who reads this book spends at least a little time thinking about this most significant topic… even those readers who believe they are already saved. It is the most important question we could ever ask about our own soul.

Am I 'SAVED'?

When I was six years old I prayed the 'sinner's prayer.'[23] Something amazing really happened to me then. That is the moment when I was sealed with the Holy Spirit and officially joined the body of Christ. I *was* changed forever and totally in love with Jesus at that young age. I know that it was something *real* because I know how it changed me. Even through the many years I ran from God, I still could feel His Holy Spirit in my soul calling me to Himself. I could not get away from the Holy Spirit, no matter how hard I ran, because He was *within me,* dwelling within my spirit. I know this because it was my own personal experience.

---

[23] *The most basic version of the sinner's prayer goes like this: "Lord Jesus, I'm a sinner. I believe You died for my sins so I could be forgiven. I receive You as my Lord and Savior. Thank You for coming into my life. Amen."*

Others looking at me from the outside during those terrible years would never have imagined that I was already a child of the King, bought with the blood of Christ. I didn't even completely understand that myself until years later.

The first point I want to make is that only Jesus truly knows our hearts. He is working in our spirits, behind the scenes, in ways other people may never see. My life is evidence of this. We must be careful of judging the salvation status of others. That is the business of God alone. Only God, through His Holy Word Jesus, is able to accurately "judge the thoughts and intentions of the heart."[24] Looks can often be very deceiving!

Our responsibility to judge someone's salvation includes only the status of *our own souls*. That's it. We are accountable to God for our own salvation, no one else's. We cannot save anyone else. We can pray for them. We can witness to them. Most importantly we can *love* them with the love of Jesus. Only they themselves can decide to receive the saving grace of the blood of Jesus Christ.

---

[24] *Hebrews 4:12 (NASB)*

WHAT IT ISN'T

So let's get down to the business of our one and only responsibility in the salvation status department... *examining our own souls.*

You either are saved or you aren't. There is no in between. There is a defining moment when salvation takes place. We aren't born with it. We must receive it through our own free will. What it looks like and the details of how it happens vary from soul to soul. It happens in one decisive moment, when your soul accepts the free gift of salvation, through the blood of Jesus Christ, and you are sealed with the Holy Spirit, forever.

If you are saved, you will probably know exactly when that happened to you. You may not have heard angels singing when it happened. You may not have jumped for joy, shouting out praises to Jesus when it happened. You may not have been slain in the spirit or spoke in tongues at the time. But you know when it happened, because something deep inside you changed.

Saying 'the sinners prayer' is not what saved me. The sinners prayer is just a bunch of words that can be repeated without understanding. Any person is able to mindlessly read the sinner's prayer off a piece of paper, or repeat the words after someone, without any change whatsoever happening in their souls.

The sinner's prayer was popularized by Billy Graham[25] in the 1970s. And ever since, all good evangelicals have run around trying to get everyone to *just say the sinners prayer*. Millions of people have now been taught that simply saying these words will save them.

I love Billy Graham. He was a great man of God and I'm sure He is supping with Jesus Christ in glory this very minute. However I believe Billy Graham's teaching on this matter has been taken out of context. And it has created a lot of confusion about what it means to be *saved*.

This sinner's prayer is not found anywhere in the Bible. I don't think there's anything *wrong* with the sinner's prayer. It is a fantastic tool. Our own pastor uses it every Sunday. But just saying those words does not save you. Saying words is an action, a 'work.' And Paul makes it clear that "it is by *grace* you have been saved, *through faith*—and this is not from yourselves, it is the *gift of God*--not by works*, so that no one can boast."[26]

None of the other 'works' that some denominations push— going to church, being confirmed or baptized—save anyone

---

[25] *If by the slightest chance there might be a reader unfamiliar with this most famous preacher, Billy Graham was a baptist preacher/evangelist whose ministry spanned 60 years from the 1940s to 2000.*

[26] *Ephesians 2:8-9 (NIV)*

either. Actual salvation is much deeper than that. It is a state of the spirit. It is a free gift from God through Jesus' death on the cross and resurrection. We cannot earn it or buy it. We can only accept and receive it.

The danger is that some people will believe they are saved simply because they repeated those words, or went through confirmation, or got baptized, or go to church. But their souls have never gone through any sort of actual transformation. They don't have the benefit of the Holy Spirit dwelling within them. They aren't saved. But they think they are, and that is a dangerous place to be. They don't bother to examine the state of their own soul because they've been taught that all they needed to do was say those words (or get baptized, or go to church, or get confirmed, or whatever other work their denomination pushes).

Is this a valid fear? Jesus makes it clear that there are many unsaved people who *think* they are saved:

> *"Not everyone who says to me, 'Lord, Lord,' will enter the kingdom of heaven, but only the one who does the will of my Father who is in heaven. Many will say to me on that day, 'Lord, Lord, did we not prophesy in your name and in your name drive out demons and in your name perform many miracles?' Then I will tell them plainly, 'I never knew you. Away from me, you evildoers!' Matthew 7:21-23 (NIV)*

Notice that these deluded people performed great works. They prophesied, drove out demons and performed miracles. I bet some of them even repeated the sinners prayer, went to church and got baptized or confirmed. Still Jesus says He never knew them. Our actions cannot save us, no matter how amazing they are.

So yes, this is a valid concern. We *really* do need to spend some time examining our own souls, even (especially) if we *think* we are saved.

WHAT MUST I DO TO BE SAVED?

So how, exactly, does one go about getting 'saved'?

To answer that question, we must go to the source, the *only true source.* Jesus Christ Himself. We must examine Jesus' words. How does Jesus *know* us? How do we ensure He will not be telling us 'I never knew you'?

Jesus said:

> *"I tell you, whoever publicly acknowledges Me before others, the Son of Man will also acknowledge before the angels of God." Luke 12:8 (NIV)*

So there you go! "Publicly acknowledge' Jesus… Is that all there is to it? Hold on a minute… whenever we really need to dig deeply into the meanings behind Jesus' words, we have to go back to the original Greek language that the New Testament was written in.[27] Unfortunately important meanings can sometimes be 'lost in translation.' Often our English language is not precise enough to completely capture the original meaning. Rest assured, the Holy Bible is living, active, and powerful in *any* language. But since the question of salvation is the most important question we could ever ask, we should probably do some digging!

The King James Version of this verse says, "Whosoever shall *confess* Me before men…" When we think of confessing or publicly acknowledging, our English brains think about spoken words. This is likely where the entire idea for a 'sinners prayer' came from. But when Jesus actually said these words to a huge crowd of people, their 1st century Jewish brains understood something much more complex. The original word in Luke's account for 'confess' is homologeó (hom-o-log-eh'-o) which meant:

> *to assent, covenant, acknowledge - profess,*
> *confession is made, give thanks promise. (combination*
> *of: homou - at the same place or time together; and*

---

[27] *Have no fear, there are now easy-to-use tools to help us do this. I recommend the Strong's Concordance. There is a free Strong's Concordance app and many free online tools available.*

logos - something said, including thought, a topic, subject of discourse, reasoning, the mental faculty, motive, computation, Divine Expression (Christ), account, cause, communication X concerning doctrine, fame X have to do, intent, matter, mouth, preaching, question, reason + reckon, remove, saying, show X speaker, speech, talk, thing + none of these things move me, tidings, treatise, utterance, word, work. (Strong's Concordance, 3670)

Sorry for the long boring definition, but you get the picture. When Jesus said "confess Me before men," He wasn't just talking about saying some predetermined words. He was pretty much talking about every single thing about a person, their entire identity, thoughts, and motives.

To *homologeó* Jesus means to undergo an *entire shift in our identity and existence.*

Have you experienced that?

Let's look again at Matthew 7:21 where Jesus explains that there will be people who think they are saved but are not, "Not everyone who says to me, 'Lord, Lord,' will enter the kingdom of heaven, but only the one who does the will of my Father who is in heaven." What does it mean to "do the will of My Father who is in heaven"? It's pretty important because Jesus says those are the only people who will "enter the kingdom of heaven!"

First of all, consider that word "do." We know salvation is a free gift, not earned through our works. So why is Jesus saying we must "do" something? The word used in Matthew is actually poieō (poy-eh'-o) which means not only to "make or do" but also to

> "abide + agree appoint X avenge + band together be bear + bewray bring (forth) cast out cause commit + continue deal + without any delay (would) do (-ing) execute exercise fulfil gain give have hold X journeying keep + lay wait + lighten the ship make X mean + none of these things move me observe ordain perform provide + have purged purpose put + raising up X secure shew X shoot out spend take tarry + transgress the law work yield." (Strong's Concordance G4160)

Hmmm that sounds a lot like what it means to "confess" (homologeó) that we examined a few paragraphs ago. Jesus was talking about much more than just doing something. He was talking about our entire identity, our motivations, purposes, and beliefs.

And just what is this "will" of God that we are supposed to poieō? The word "will" is thelēma (thel'-ay-mah) - "a determination (properly the thing) that is (actively) choice (specifically purpose decree; abstractly volition) or (passively) inclination: - desire pleasure will."[28] So basically God's "will" is whatever He desires for us to poieō.

---

28 *Strong's Concordance G2307*

So what does God desire us to do???

Well guess what, God Himself actually *tells* us what it is that He wants us to do, in His own voice, in the New Testament.

God speaks directly to us twice in the gospels. The first time is when Jesus is baptized[29] and the second is at the Transfiguration when Peter, James, and John see Jesus in His glorified form.[30]

Both times God says the exact same thing, "This is my beloved Son, in whom I am well pleased." The second time He adds a command to "Listen to Him!"

So first God identifies Jesus for us and then He tells us what to do about it.

Jesus then conveniently tells us exactly what it is that we are supposed to do, a bunch of times, in a variety of different ways, just to make sure that we all get it. We've already looked at two of those instances in this chapter when Jesus explains who knows Him and who enters the kingdom of heaven.

Jesus explains what exactly is the will of God in this passage from John:

---

[29] *Matthew 3:13-17*

[30] *Matthew 17:1-13*

"For this is the will of My Father, that everyone who looks on the Son and believes in Him should have eternal life, and I will raise Him up on the last day."
John 6:40 (ESV)

So yep, now we have to pick it apart a bit.

What does it mean to "look on the Son?" The word here is theōreō (theh-o-reh'-o) which means to "see, behold, perceive, consider, look on."[31] Okay so everyone who thinks about Jesus must do what?

"Believe in Him."

This word for "believe" is pisteuō (pit-yoo'-o) which goes much deeper than just believing something like 'the sky is blue' or '2 + 2 = 4.'

Pisteuō means:

> *"to have faith (in upon or with respect to a person or thing) that is credited; by implication to entrust (especially one's spiritual well being to Christ): - believe (-r) commit (to trust) put in trust with." (Strong's Concordance, G4100)*

---

[31] *Strong's Concordance, G2334*

We must have faith in who Jesus is (the Son of God) and trust the state of our souls to Him.

Have you done that?

I'll finish up with John 3, the chapter in the Bible that includes John 3:16, which you probably know by heart even if you never tried to memorize it, because it is the most often quoted verse in the entire Bible. And there is a reason for that. The third chapter of John contains the most clear and concise explanation of how to get saved in the whole of Scripture. If you ask me what is the most important chapter in the entire Bible, I would tell you John 3. It deserves a bit more of our attention.

JOHN 3

In the third chapter of John, a Pharisee named Nicodemus has a secret meeting with Jesus.

Here is Jesus' opportunity to go really deep. Did you ever notice how differently Jesus speaks to the Pharisees than He does to all the other people? Jesus was a masterful communicator. He changed His language and approach depending upon who His audience was.

To the masses, He spoke in parables, simple stories about situations from their daily lives to teach them underlying truths about the Kingdom of God. Jesus wasn't speaking down to them, or insinuating that they were stupid. He was engaging them in a way that they could easily *relate* to. Their lives were simple lives of sustenance — farmers, shepherds, and fishermen — and Jesus met them there in His stories.

The religious leaders were very different. Their lives were consumed with books, learning, and theology, rather than manual labor for sustenance. So when Jesus spoke to them, He delved into the realm of the philosophical rather than parables. His explanation of salvation to Nicodemus is much more cerebral than the life stories He uses with the others.

He tells Nicodemus, "Very truly I tell you, no one can see the kingdom of God unless they are born again."[32]

Nicodemus asks, "How can someone be born when they are old? ... Surely they cannot enter a second time into their mother's womb to be born!"[33]

Jesus responds:

> "Very truly I tell you, no one can enter the kingdom of God unless they are born of water and the Spirit. Flesh

---

[32] *v. 3*

[33] *v. 4*

*gives birth to flesh, but the Spirit gives birth to spirit.
You should not be surprised at my saying, 'You must
be born again.' The wind blows wherever it pleases.
You hear its sound, but you cannot tell where it comes
from or where it is going. So it is with everyone born of
the Spirit."[34]*

"How can this be?" Nicodemus asks.

Jesus answers:

*"You are Israel's teacher… and you do not understand
these things? Very truly I tell you, we speak of what we
know, and we testify to what we have seen, but still you
people do not accept our testimony. I have spoken to
you of earthly things and you do not believe; how then
will you believe if I speak of heavenly things? No one
has ever gone into heaven except the one who came
from heaven—the Son of Man. Just as Moses lifted up
the snake in the wilderness, so the Son of Man must
be lifted up, that everyone who believes may have
eternal life in Him. For God so loved the world that He
gave His one and only Son, that whoever believes in
Him shall not perish but have eternal life. For God did
not send His Son into the world to condemn the world,
but to save the world through Him. Whoever believes in
Him is not condemned, but whoever does not believe*

---

[34] *vs. 5-8*

stands condemned already because they have not
believed in the name of God's one and only Son."[35]

Everyone knows John 3:16 but many don't know the context in which it was spoken. Jesus drops all the stories with Nicodemus and speaks plainly. This is it, once and for all, the most clearly stated explanation from Jesus about what is required for salvation in the Bible.

Volumes of books are needed to properly break this all down. I just want to point out a few things. When Jesus says "whoever believes in Him shall not perish but have eternal life," that word "believes" is pisteuō[36] again that we saw in Matthew 7.

Jesus says that everyone who pisteuō in Him will not perish *(the word for perish is apollumi - to destroy fully, lose, be lost[37])* but will live forever. He states this same idea four times in four different ways *(verses 15, 16, 17, and 18)* to make sure Nicodemus understands this is important.

In verse 17 He clearly says that God sent Him "into the world [not] to condemn the world, but to save the world *through*

---

[35] *vs. 10-18*

[36] *Once more pisteuō means: "to have faith (in upon or with respect to a person or thing) that is credit; by implication to entrust (especially one's spiritual well being to Christ): - believe (-r) commit (to trust) put in trust with." (Strong's Concordance, G4100)*

[37] *Strong's Concordance G622*

146

Him." The word for "save" is sōzō (which means "to save that is to deliver or protect (literally or figuratively): - heal preserve save (self) do well be (make) whole."[38]

Everyone who pisteuō Jesus will be made whole and live forever!

One final point is that Jesus clearly states that believing in Him is the only way to salvation.

Verse 17 tells us that God sent Jesus "to save the world *through Him.*" That word "through" is dia *(dee-ah')* and it is a preposition that means exactly the same thing as our English word *(finally!)* which is "the channel of an act."[39] So the world is saved *through* the channel of Jesus' death and resurrection.[40]

In verse 18, Jesus says "whoever does not believe stands condemned already because they have not believed in the name of God's one and only Son." Whoever, anyone, everyone who does *not* pisteuō Jesus is what? Jesus says they are already "condemned." That word is krinō (kree'-no)

---

[38] *Strong's Concordance G4982*

[39] *Strong's Concordance G1223*

[40] *So please do not be seduced by this false idea that has crept into many churches that there are many ways to salvation. That ideology is completely opposite to what Jesus has said.*

which means "properly to distinguish that is decide (mentally or judicially); by implication to try condemn punish: - avenge conclude condemn damn decree determine esteem judge go to (sue at the) law ordain call in question sentence to think."[41]

So everyone who does not pisteuō Jesus will not only be judged and punished but their judgement is in the past tense. It has *already* happened. And the condemnation is *their own decision*, not something God is imposing upon them.

Make sense?

We decide our own fate. Jesus doesn't decide for us. God doesn't *send* anybody to hell. He lets us choose where we want to go. God provided the way to salvation, which is Jesus. All we have to do is pisteuō Jesus to receive salvation. It is a free gift! But God won't force salvation upon us. We have to choose it. Our relationship to Jesus is the most important decision we could ever make.

WHAT ARE YOU GOING TO DO ABOUT IT?

So now is the time to examine your soul. If you do not feel the presence of the Holy Spirit in your soul, if you aren't aware of Him tugging at your heart, calling you to Himself, it is possible

---

[41] *Strong's Concordance G2919*

that He is not there. You can fix that in a moment by humbly asking Jesus to save you.

On the other hand, if you feel drawn to Jesus, if you love Him and want to know Him more, then you don't need to be fearful about this. It is impossible to love and follow Jesus without the Holy Spirit's presence. You are good! Let's get on with the process of learning to utilize all the marvelous privileges that are given to us when we are saved.

CASH IN YOUR BENEFITS!

Salvation is free and quick. That's the easy part! You don't have to work for it and you can't earn it. All you have to do is just want it and ask for it. Then Jesus adds your name to His Book of Life and imparts the Holy Spirit into you. He puts His mark on your soul and you are joined to His Holy Spirit forever. Your eternity is now secure. You will spend it with God and Jesus and all the angels and all the other saved souls in a glorious place called heaven. You are saved! YAY! You have your heaven ticket.

What now? Some people just shove that heaven ticket in their back pocket and continue on with their lives just as before. People who do that spiritually sleepwalk through their lives. They struggle with all the fears, depressions, and anxieties that other people do. Their eternal destination may have changed but nothing else ever does. They may wonder why this Christianity thing never really did anything for them, if they even think about it at all.

Paul talks about people like this in his letter to the Corinthians. They are "people who are still worldly—mere infants in Christ" who are not yet ready for "solid food."[42] He urges them to "build with care" because a day is coming when their "work will be shown for what it is."[43] There will be Christians, Paul warns, whose whole lives will count for nothing. All their works will be burned up. They will be saved. They have their heaven ticket afterall. But "only as one escaping through the flames."[44] This is the saddest fate for a Christian, totally avoidable and unnecessary.

Being saved can be much more than just a heaven ticket… infinitely more. The Bible is filled with all the promises, fruit of the spirit, authority, victory, wholeness, and well-being, and so much more that is granted to us after we are saved. These are benefits of our salvation that are available to us right here *right now*.

However just as God won't force salvation upon us, He won't *make* us use all these benefits either. He insists upon giving us free will to the very end. How tragic it is that many Christians

---

[42] *1 Corinthians 3:1-2 (NIV)*

[43] *1 Corinthians 3:10-13 (NIV)*

[44] *1 Corinthians 3:14 (NIV)*

never reap the possible rewards of salvation in this life. So many Christians continue living defeated, fearful, depressed, unhealthy lives until they die. Don't be that person.

Have you ever known a Christian who is so full of love, joy and peace that it just bubbles out of them? It's not just their personality, or something they were born with. Living a life of love, joy and peace is available to *every single person* who is saved through Jesus.

Every. Single. Person.

God *promises* to give us these things and so much more!

So how to we cash in on our benefits? There is a process to it. It doesn't just come naturally to us. We have to learn how to do it. Yes you have to do a little work to get there. The work is actually what teaches you how so it can't be skipped. There aren't any shortcuts but it is so worth the work. The process is called sanctification which means 'the process of becoming/making holy.' Sanctification is the journey we take to become more like Jesus Christ.

I call it becoming spiritually awake.

Let's wake up!

WAKING UP

Getting saved, by having faith in who Jesus is (the Son of God) and trusting the state of your soul to Him, is the *first, most important, necessary* step. Without salvation, you have no access to the Holy Spirit's working or all the many promises of God. So please make sure you've taken care of that first step!

After your salvation has been assured, you are ready to embark upon the journey of sanctification. Your spirit can now begin the process of fully waking up, drawing closer to and becoming more like Jesus.

When we get saved, our spiritual identities change. One of the most amazing gifts Jesus gives us when we receive Him is this new identity. We no longer must be victims in this hard world, helpless against abuse, slaves to our own fears.

> *"So you are no longer a slave, but God's child; and since you are His child, God has made you also an heir." Galatians 4:7*

Jesus gives us a new identity of royalty, victorious overcomer, loved, chosen, strong. As children of the King we are heirs with Jesus Christ, seated at the right hand of God![45] We will reign

---

[45] *Ephesians 2:6*

152

in heaven with Jesus Christ for all eternity. And it is going to be glorious!

There is so much more. Jesus proclaimed that the Kingdom of Heaven is "at hand." That means it is available to us right now, in this life. The Bible is filled with promises that we can access right now. All of the promises in the Bible are proof to us that God loves us and wants to be in relationship with us now, while we are still in this life. God desires for us to grow closer to Him and to reap all of the benefits our salvation status offers us. We don't have to wait until we get to heaven to enjoy our new identities in Christ.

God doesn't force this new identity upon us. We must learn how to live this new amazing way. He will lead us into that new wonderful life if we only follow Him. We do that by desiring to know Him better, and doing things that will help make that happen — things like prayer, worship, Bible reading, meeting with other Christians who also want to grow closer to God. We don't do these things to 'follow the rules' but out of the desire of our hearts to grow closer to Jesus. In my own life, meditative prayer has been a core ingredient to deepening my relationship with God. Meditative prayer has awakened my spirit to God more than anything else in my life.

Paul talks about the Holy Spirit as a pledge or a deposit of our inheritance.[46] When we want to buy a house, we usually have to give a deposit, earnest money, to hold the property and

---

[46] *2 Corinthians 1:21-22 & Ephesians 1:14*

prove that we are serious about buying the house. The Holy Spirit's presence in us as believers works in a similar way. It not only seals (stamps) us with God's approval to mark us as God's property, but also is proof to us that our salvation is real and that God means business. The Holy Spirit helps us and teaches us as we work to get closer to God. Our faith grows stronger and our spirit comes more alive as we experience the Holy Spirit's presence within us.

When I became a Christian at six years old, I began my own personal intimate relationship with God. My spirit began this process of waking up. I did fall back asleep spiritually during the many years I ran away from God. But the Holy Spirit never left me. Seeds of that spiritual awakening were always deep down in my soul. Every time I came back to God, to Jesus, my first love, my spirit awakened a little more. I was always so miserable during the times in my life when I was far from God because the Holy Spirit within me was always nudging my spirit, calling me, trying to woo me back to Himself *(thank You, Jesus!)*. The harder I tried to run away from that small voice within my soul, the more miserable I became. For a child of God, there simply is no true joy or peace without communion with Jesus.

When my car ran off the road and God told me that was the last time I would ever be spared, my soul blasted awake. I finally committed to holding on to Jesus and work to grow closer to Him. And as long as I continue seeking God and working to grow closer to Him I never will fall back asleep.

CAN I JUST GO TO CHURCH?

Sadly, for many Christians, the extent of their connection with God rests solely upon church attendance. As long as their bottoms occupy a pew occasionally, they assume they are doing this Christianity thing, but it isn't personal or meaningful in any way. They never invest in a real relationship with Jesus and so there is never any sort of spiritual awakening. Are people like this really saved? That is only for God to judge! All I know is that their Christianity isn't doing very much for them. Their lives are no different than non-believers. They certainly aren't enjoying any of the benefits that salvation offers.

Going to church does not save us.

Many people do find God at church. Our pastor has a powerful anointing for evangelism, and people get saved at our church every single week. Many people learn about Jesus and the Bible and experience true life-changing salvation in church. I learned about Jesus in Sunday School as a child. Church is where most real Christians connect with each other and experience true fellowship and the presence of God. Yes, many many people find God at church.

A lot of people don't.

I've observed that having an intimate relationship with God and organized Christianity don't always co-exist.

Many of the people I grew up with in Southern Baptist church were delightfully and obviously deeply in love with God; Holy Spirit joy just oozed out of them.

Others, even some church leaders, did not appear to have relationship with God at all. Many of them were angry, spiteful, bitter people. Some of them did horrible evil things. I've met a lot of people who identify themselves as Christians but are hateful or chronically depressed or full of fear and self-loathing or worse. Their Christianity hasn't helped them to wake up spiritually. Much of today's organized Christianity has become a culture, a set of rules that can be followed without anything spiritual ever happening inside the individual. This is exactly the same accusation Jesus made of the Pharisees.

I'm not telling anyone not to go to church. It is extremely important to connect with other Christians. We make up the body of Christ. We need each other. And the best way to do that is by finding a good church. Just be aware that some churches are run by people who are very much spiritually asleep. Use discernment and seek God's guidance when choosing your church. Look for a church that is vibrant and alive, a home full of people who are also in love with Jesus Christ where the Bible is taught and your soul can be nourished.

THE ANESTHESIA OF LEGALISM

There is no more powerful soul-killer than legalism. Watch out for this tricky evil spirit as you are awakening your soul. I grew up in an overly legalistic church denomination and I have seen first hand the dangers of legalistic spirits. Christians under the spell of legalism fixate upon following a set of rules. Christianity to them is a cold formulaic system rather than a life-giving relationship with Jesus Christ. *(They are pretty easy to recognize because they are usually joyless and stern. They are the trolls on Christian social media groups starting arguments with everyone.)* They try to force the yoke of law around the necks of everyone else within their grasp. They demand strict adherence to whatever is their narrow definition of the *'correct' way* to be a Christian. And there are endless definitions to choose from in the world of legalistic Christianity. Don't get caught in this never ending trap.

Live in spiritual freedom, not legalism. We don't have to fret about being theologically correct about *every single little detail*. If God requires perfect theology then we're *all* doomed. That would require us to be perfect and all-knowing. It's pretty obvious that humans are neither of those things. We are fallible imperfect creatures. No one of us can be totally correct about *everything*. Our brains are just too finite to completely comprehend the infinite. Only God knows it all. And we miss intimacy with God when we are fearful about finding the *perfect* theology or when we waste precious energy persecuting others who don't exactly agree with details of our particular theology. Don't worry about all that stuff. Just seek Jesus! Work to have a relationship with Jesus. Your true healing is there in His loving embrace.

I am a Christian. I believe Christianity is the way God has ordained as a bridge from us to Himself. I believe that God decided how He wanted to reach out to us and then gave us a book to explain it. God *is* bigger than the institution of Christianity. I believe that Jesus Christ is the only way to get to God, but it is only because that is how *God decided* to set it all up. God is the ultimate truth and He has the power, and the right, to decide however He wants to do things. He is, and always will be, in charge of all of this. We are, and will always be (while we are in these cursed physical bodies), too dense to really understand it all. And if we recognize our own fallibility, it should help us to extend love towards people who don't believe exactly the same way that we do.

Getting closer to God isn't a set of rules. It is a *personal relationship*. No one else can have a relationship with Jesus *for you*. No one can tell you exactly how God will work in your life, in your particular situation. It's up to *you* to seek God and listen to what He will tell you. There are a million different ways He might choose to work with you. God is that infinite. If God is immense enough to know each one of us personally (and I believe He is) then He is big enough to customize a unique path for every single one of us to get to know Him. God speaks to all of us if we listen. *All* of us. God speaks to us in a million different ways. He gives some people visions. He gives other people dreams. To others He speaks in a still small voice. To others He gives signs. You only need to find the path that God wants *you* to travel.

I believe that organized Christianity goes astray when people try to put rules on finding God based upon the specific way that God has chosen to work with them. This assumes that whatever singular way God has worked with a particular individual is the way God would choose to work with everyone. This just can't be correct. God is so immense and complex. Just a cursory glimpse at creation demonstrates His love for variety.

Organizing a system of rules removes God from the equation. Once you have steps to follow, it becomes just following steps rather than seeking the Creator of the Universe. God cannot be put into the box of a denomination. God cannot be summarized or defined by a theology.

Millions of people grow up thinking that God is contained in the tenets of whatever their denomination affiliation is. They believe that God only works in the narrow way their particular denomination teaches. And when God doesn't work in exactly that way, they miss God's work. They don't recognize that God is all around them and within them, working and communicating constantly. If I had only been taught to *seek* God *first* rather than to follow a system of rules, I could have been saved from many years of spiritual staleness and rebellion. Growing close to God is a process and everyone must work their way through it for themselves. Blessed are those who continue to seek until they really find God.

BE STILL AND KNOW THAT I AM GOD

Like Elijah, I found God in meditation and quietness, in "a still small voice"[47] that had previously been drowned out by our noisy culture, and my own incessant thoughts. Meditation allowed me to just come to God for the first time in my life completely open, with no filters or expectations. Meditation allowed me to quiet down my brain and emotions so that God could really communicate with my soul. Meditation allowed me to really meet with God.

I used to do religious things because I thought I was supposed to do them... go to church, memorize scripture, read the Bible, witness to people, sing praise songs, etc. The closer I get to God the more all of that is turned upside down. Those are all very good things, and useful tools, but they cannot replace real relationship with God. The relationship part must come first. Everything else should be a response and outpouring of that love relationship.

To know God is to love God. The more we know God, the more we worship Him. The knowing and the worshipping are one and the same.

When I grew up I always felt that worship was something I had to make myself feel, to work up a worshipful feeling within my emotions, because I thought it was what I was *supposed* to do.

---

[47] *1 Kings 19:12 KJV*

That was before I began to really know God. True worship is spontaneous response to the glorious wonderfulness of God. It cannot be stopped. To be fully spiritually awake, to *know* God, is to worship God — the spontaneous natural response when we glimpse the amazingness of God is worship.

In one way we humans are small, insignificant, often dumb creatures. But we are also loved by the Creator of the Universe. How amazing is that? And this Creator of the Universe is calling us, wooing us, drawing us. God *is* real and wants to have a relationship with us and that is the most beautiful, fantastic thing.

There is so much joy to be accessed within our souls if we only understand that God, the Creator of the cosmos, knows and loves each one of us individually. We are in the middle of a glorious love story. And we already know that it ends happily ever after. It really does. But in the meantime, we have much work to do. We must pray for the world to understand this, for more and more people to wake up to this truth. God really loves us. God desires to call *all* souls into an intimate relationship with Himself.

THE VASTNESS OF GOD

God is everywhere. His divine fingerprints are imprinted on His entire creation. God is working everywhere, in every place, person, heart and mind... in a zillion different ways... whether people see it or not, God is always present. "If I go up to the heavens, [God is] there; if I make my bed in the depths, [God is] there."[48] We only have to open our eyes and look for God. We only need to seek God and He will meet us some how, some way. When we seek God with our whole hearts, we will find Him.[49]

I believe that God is in charge of this entire human physical parade from beginning to end. God will decide if, when, were, what and how. *However*... even though God is in control, usually *we* have to make some sort of effort to seek Him out. My observation has been that God doesn't often *force* people to wake up. We have to *try*. We have to create extra space in our life to meet with Him. The most important thing that is up to *you* is whether or not you will acknowledge God and try to get closer to Him. That is the *one thing* you control. Get that part right.

So *how* do you try? Just *wanting* to find God is a pretty good indicator that you are on the road to spiritual awakening

---

48 Psalm 139:8 NIV

49 Jeremiah 29:13 NIV

already. Probably that's why you even considered reading this book. If this is something you are wanting, all I can tell you is to seek God some how, some way. If you want to hear God's voice, you have to stop the noise… all the external noises and your own thoughts fighting for your attention. Read the Bible. Get quiet. Turn off your tv. Get off social media. Meditate. Pray. Be still. If you do that consistently, and your motivation is to grow nearer to God, He *will* begin to reveal Himself to you some how, some way.

I can't tell you exactly what that is going to look like in your life. No one can tell you that. And don't let anyone try. This has to be *your* journey. You and God. Nobody can do it for you. And no one can really tell you specifically how to do it either because every journey is different. The answer is there if you look for it in the quiet depths of your soul, if you will only be still and seek Him.

FINDING JESUS.

God is the highest, most complex entity in existence. His thoughts and ways are so much higher than ours.[50] Our human brains will never be able to completely understand Him. That is why He put so much effort into providing a comprehensive written letter, the Bible, to help us understand those things He wants us to know.

The Bible is a miraculous divine book. It was written by over 40 different authors spanning 1500 years. Yet the entire book points to one singular theme… Jesus Christ. The Bible is where we learn about Jesus. The more we learn about Jesus, the more we will understand about God and His ways.

The closer I get to God, the more He points me to his son, Jesus. God chose to come to earth in the human form of Jesus Christ in order to defeat the curse of death and allow us to commune intimately with Him. God chose Jesus to be the bridge between His perfect self and us fallen humans. Any discussion about finding God is incomplete without acknowledging the way God has selected for us to find Him. We dare not attempt to leave Jesus out of this system of salvation. Attempting to forge a relationship with God without Jesus will be incomplete.

---

[50] *Isaiah 55:8-9*

When Jesus heals the paralyzed man who was lowered through the ceiling, he first told the man that his sins were forgiven. Jesus knew the thoughts of the teachers of the law who heard Him say this and He told them "Which is easier: to say to this paralyzed man, 'Your sins are forgiven,' or to say, 'Get up, take your mat and walk?' But I want you to know that the Son of Man has authority on earth to forgive sins." So He said to the man, "I tell you, get up, take your mat and go home," He got up, took his mat and walked out in full view of them all.[51] Do you see what Jesus did there? He first said that He had the power to forgive sins and then offered proof of this by physically healing the paralytic. Words are cheap. Jesus backed up his claim with physical proof.

Jesus' words in this story show us the two different identities of Christ, God and man. When Jesus was on earth, he existed completely in both the spiritual and physical realms.

As God, Jesus was always fully engaged in the spiritual realm. He knew people's thoughts and communicated with demons and angels. Mark tells us that "whenever the impure spirits saw [Jesus], they fell down before him, and cried out, 'You are the Son of God.'"[52] The demons, who also exist in the spiritual realm, saw and recognized the deity of Jesus. As God, Jesus could spiritually heal and forgive sins.

---

[51] *Mark 2:1-12 NIV*

[52] *Mark 3:11 NIV*

As a human, Jesus could interact with us physically. Jesus the physical man performed countless physical miracles that were a parallel to what He could also do in the spiritual realm. His physical miracles were visual proof of his spiritual authority, since the purely spiritual miracles, such as forgiving sins and saving people's souls, were invisible.

While Christ walked the earth physically, He healed people physically. As the Son of Man, Christ is our physical healer. Any physical healing we receive in this life will only be temporary since we all eventually will physically die. But His spiritual healings endure. The spiritual component of Christ, the Holy Spirit, continues the personal work of Christ today in the spiritual realm.

True eternal healing happens inside our souls. Spiritual healings are eternal just as our souls are eternal. I believe that authentic healing from depression must address the spiritual level to be true and lasting.

When people asked Jesus why his disciples did not fast, he answered, "How can guests of the bridegroom fast while he is with them? They cannot, so long as they have Him with them. But the time will come when the bridegroom will be taken from them, and on that day they will fast."[53] Those three short years of Jesus' ministry changed everything. When He was with us, as one of us, we had the luxury of His physical presence. What a blessed time. Every place He went, He healed the sick

---

[53] *Mark 2: 18-20*

and the lame, and cast out demons. He was physically demonstrating to us His great power visually so that we might recognize His spiritual authority.

Now we are in a season when the physical Jesus is no longer with us. Now is a season when we have the Holy Spirit with us and His spiritual work *is* promised. The Holy Spirit often works in the physical realm today, but He *always* works in the spiritual realm.

When Jesus touched people they were healed. Just touching His physical body cured their own bodies. The physical presence of Jesus brought people closer to their glorified selves… to the immortal bodies that wait for us on the other side of the veil… the perfect glorious bodies of Adam and Eve before the fall. God cannot wait to give us these amazing bodies!

Jesus physically healed everyone He encountered but that was not His reason for coming to us as a human. Jesus told His first disciples that His reason for coming to us was to preach, "Let's go on to the neighboring villages so that I may preach there too. This is why I have come."[54] He came here to tell and show us the way to God. The physical healings were the visual proof of the power Jesus had to spiritually heal. I believe Jesus also *wanted* to heal when He encountered hurting people. He had so much compassion for everyone He met.

---

[54] *Mark 1:38 CSB*

I believe Jesus does want to heal us spiritually. He has as much compassion for us today as He demonstrated when he walked among us in human form. If we seek Him, ask Him for healing, and agree to do whatever He calls us to do to get to that healing, He will indeed spiritually heal us.

In Mark we read that twice Jesus miraculously multiplied bread and fish to feed the multitudes. Later when the disciples worried about having forgotten to bring bread, Jesus asked them, "Do you still not understand?"[55] They had watched Jesus heal physically broken bodies, turn water to wine, create food from nothing. Yet still they worried about physical bread.

As God, outside of time, existing in the spiritual realm, Jesus was never constrained by physical limitations. Rules of physics did not apply to Him. How insignificant this physical world is when compared to God. We will all understand this the instant we are confronted with God's mighty presence after we leave these physical bodies. All of our years of toil and trouble, plans and dreams will vanish in an instant like a puff of smoke. And we'll be left with nothing but our souls and be able to do nothing else but to scream out "I had no idea! I had no idea!" *(I had a vision of this moment!)*

Jesus' death on the cross was so much more, so much deeper than His blood covering our sin as I was taught growing up. Jesus was God. And God *became* man so that God as man

---

[55] *Mark 8:17 NIV*

could die for us to connect us to God. The only way to get to God is to die because God is spirit. Our cursed physical bodies separate us from Him. We only become completely spirit after we die and shed this physical body. *That* is why death is required. Before Jesus came, sacrifices of animals were a temporary replacement for our own required death. Jesus' death was the ultimate sacrifice that covers us all forever *while we are in this physical body*. Jesus' sacrifice is not just a cover for sin but also a release from this physical body into the spirit realm.

And the whole idea of sin is so much different than what I was taught growing up. Sin isn't just telling a lie or taking a cookie when mom told you not to. We've turned this concept of sin into something so shallow. Sin is actually this entire physical world. Sin is the curse placed on Adam and Eve and their descendants when they forged their contract with Satan. *Sin is everything physical.* It is all rotting away because it is all cursed. It is all *sin*. It is all trapped within *time* which is also part of the curse. Time is what had to be broken open by God becoming man and dying once and for all so that we might be connected to God while still in this physical life of sin.

If you love your life and the things of this world too much… you are investing your heart in temporary decaying things. God became one of these foul rotting things to draw us to Himself. God came to us as one of us so that we could see and know God. Jesus needed to enter into our cursed physical world in order for us to perceive Him. Our temporal rotting bodies will always conclude in death (unless Jesus returns first). But

Christ came back from the dead. Even as a human, death could not keep Christ.

SATAN

God gave instructions to the Israelites for sacrifices "so that the glory of the LORD may appear to you."[56] Sacrifices were required because of the curse. They were not needed before the fall. Before the fall of man, there was no death. When Adam and Eve sinned, they entered into a contract with Satan for all of mankind. God created mankind to have dominion and rule over the earth. But Adam and Eve sold their birthright *(just as Esau did[57])* of earthly dominion to the enemy. They accepted Satan's terms and we have been under the curse of this sin covenant ever since. With it came death and the curse of time and our exile within these rotting bodies.

I've seen demons. I know they are real. Jesus agrees with me about that. Jesus cast demons out of people in every town he visited. He didn't counsel them about their childhood or give them Prozac. He cast demons out of them. I know that demonic possession and oppression exist. It is probably much more prevalent than people in our postmodern science age suspect. I believe that many people suffer from demonic

---

[56] *Leviticus 9:6 NIV*

[57] *Genesis 25:27-34*

oppression today. Satan owns this world and his legions of demons are everywhere, all around us. Of course we are affected by them. I know in my own case, my suicidal depression was a direct result of years of demonic oppression *(I believe this is probably the case for many people suffering from depression)*.

If demons are real then it follows that Satan, Beelzebub, Lucifer, the father of all lies, is also a reality. Jesus certainly believed in Satan. He talked to him and talked about him often. Immediately after Jesus was baptized (the official start of His ministry) "at once the Spirit sent Him out into the wilderness, and He was in the wilderness forty days, being tempted by Satan."[58] Before Jesus could reach us, He had to grapple with the one who is currently contractually the ruler of this world, Satan. He had to spiritually wrestle with Satan and defeat his temptations before beginning His ministry to us. Satan attempted to draw Jesus into his contractual agreement, just as he does to all of us. But Jesus defeated him.

We learn a lot about Satan in this encounter. Satan always promises us variations of the same three things:

1. A life of ease/wealth (turn stones to bread)
2. Fame/to be worshipped by man (bow to Satan and the earth would be His)
3. Control (throw Himself down from temple; this is also the lie Satan used on Eve in the Garden of Eden)

---

[58] *Mark 1:12 NIV*

These have *always* been Satan's *promises* to us from the beginning of time. They all tap into one weakness — *pride* — our cursed desire to take the place of God. It was Satan's own sin and the reason he fell. But *everything* Satan tells us is untrue. All of his promises are lies.

All of our troubles in this cursed world lead back to pride in some form... trying to replace God with something of the flesh.

Why exactly is this pride thing so terrible anyway? Why are we told to be humble?

It's not because God just wants to keep us down, or beat us up. To be truly humble is simply understanding the truth of our situation. The truth is that even the most brilliant or powerful human is still just a stupid, weak creature when compared to the Creator of the Universe. That is why God's love for us is so incredible. The almighty, omniscient, all-knowing God of the Universe *loves us*!

This is the same reason we are called to worship God. God doesn't crave or need our worship because He is some narcissistic egomaniac. To worship God is simply acknowledging the truth of how amazing God is.

Since God is the ultimate truth, these instructions to be humble and to worship God, simply align ourselves with the *truth*.

Satan is the opposite of truth. Satan creates a physical counterfeit of every holy thing God has ever created. To take anything that is connected to spirit (sex, relationships, our bodies, food, earth, etc.) and turn it into something purely physical is to turn it upside down. Satan always works by perverting the spiritual and turning it into something only physical. To worship flesh is the highest obscenity, the great idol of our 21st century culture. Nothing good can ever come of worshipping the physical. It leads us straight to a hellish existence of misery and demonic bondage.

We make horrible gods. The most unhappy, angry, fearful, judgmental people I know are people who believe that human beings are capable of perfection, that we could somehow create utopia on earth. We aren't and we can't. Only God is capable of either of those things. Once we understand this truth, we are free to be the imperfect creatures we are and to love and worship the only true perfect God.

Satan and his evil demon minions hate God. Their hatred consumes them. It motivates everything they do. They know how this story ends. They know God will be victorious and they will lose. So the only way they can get revenge is by destroying us. They know how much God loves us and they hate us because God loves us. Destroying us is the only way they can hurt God. They are trying as hard as they can to damage as many of us as possible. They know their time is limited and they are giving it all they've got.

Following God, staying close to God, will never just come naturally while we are in this world. It must be worked on, fought for, trained for with all the determined stubborn discipline of a marathon runner. We are in enemy territory in this world. Our adversary, Satan, will never give up. He will never stop opposing us or fighting against us. So we can't give up either. God will help us defend ourselves against Satan if we let Him.

MEDITATIVE PRAYER

Meditative prayer is a tool that can help teach us to differentiate mind from spirit, to separate our eternal spirit from our temporal flesh. It can be a doorway for us to tap into our spirit, our true self. It can train us to subjugate our physical self, to give our spirit control rather than our mind, body, or emotion. Meditative prayer can help us to recognize the proper place of our flesh as temporary, and much lower than our spirit. Meditative prayer can help us understand that our spirit is our highest, most important form, our true identity, the only part of us that is eternal and not part of this cursed physical world.

It is easy to tell the difference between our *spirit* and our *physical body* because they are so unlike each other. But separating our *thoughts* from our *spirit* is much more difficult. Our thoughts and spirit often seem to overlap. A good way to see the difference between the thoughts and spirit is considering the gift of tongues. When someone speaks in tongues, their spirit uses their physical body, their mouth and tongue, to speak. But the person's mind usually does not understand what their mouth is saying. Paul says that "anyone who speaks in a tongue does not speak to people but to God. Indeed, no one understands them; they utter mysteries by the Spirit."[59] In the gift of tongues we see that the spirit is able to control our physical mouth and tongue. So it follows that we can learn how to let our spirit control our physical bodies. I believe we can learn to allow our spirit to control our thoughts as well. We must first learn to discern the difference between the two.

Unfortunately it isn't an easy thing to do while we are in this physical form. It takes a lot of practice. Please believe me that it is so very worth the time and effort. I believe that learning to be still through meditative prayer is a key to emotional and spiritual wellness. I believe it is a key to healing from depression. It is a key to seeking and knowing God. It is a key to moving toward spiritual awakening.

---

[59] *1 Corinthians 14:2 NIV*

GOD'S PRESENCE

We are at such a disadvantage in our relationships with each other. We must rely on our words and actions to communicate with each other. Everything in our human relationships depends upon our actions and words. God, who knows our hearts and intentions intimately, has no such limitations. God's dealings with us can be completely pure and a true response to who we and our motivations really are. I believe our actual physical actions matter very little to God compared to the state of our hearts. God's Word (Jesus) judges the thoughts and attitudes of our heart.[60]

God is omnipresent. That means God is everywhere at all times, always present. God's presence permeates everything in the universe. Every person, animal, tree, rock, etc. holds an imprint of God. Whatever we do, wherever we go, God is there. It doesn't matter where you are… walking in the woods, driving to work, taking a shower, cooking dinner… God is always present. You are always able to tap into God's presence no matter what you are doing, or where you are as long as you seek God's companionship and are aware of His divine presence.

You can learn about the character of God by studying creation. God made all of His great creation for us to understand Him. Everything has endless meanings and parallels to God and to

---

[60] *Hebrews 4:12 NIV*

the holy spiritual realm. Just as our spirits are temporarily connected to our physical bodies during this time of exile, so too I believe there is a connected spiritual counterpart for every created thing on this earth. Everything in this universe is also currently in this same state of exile from the spiritual realm... imprisoned in this mortal decaying shell. That is why the whole creation is crying out as in birth pangs.[61]

When God created the earth, He created a physical parallel for every component of heaven, every component of Himself. The entire creation is an enormous puzzle full of clues to learn about God. How fun. And all we have to do is just pay attention and God delights to reveal these clues to us.

All of our physical senses — sound, sight, taste, smell, touch — were created for us to experience our physical world. We can only experience the *spiritual* world through our spirit. We can use our physical senses to connect to our spirits as we worship the Creator by immersing ourselves within His creation. Meditative prayer can help us learn to do this.

We've all felt the thin spaces... when our heart is stirred by a haunting song... or we are brought to tears by a spectacular sunset. These are things that move our souls... that move us more deeply than our minds and emotions. These are things that break through the physical veil to our souls and touch the eternal part of us. We've all felt it. You've felt it. You know what I'm talking about. If you can learn to do that on cue... to tap

---

[61] *Romans 8:22 NKJV*

into your own spirit, quiet your mind and calm your emotions so that your spirit can take control, to shed this rough physical shell for a few moments and step onto the other side of the veil — that is spiritual awakening, that is seeking relationship with God.

When we hear a voice sing a note that touches our soul, and sends a shiver down our bodies, that is exactly what is happening to us. That note in that moment is piercing through the veil and touching your soul. That is exactly the substance of my visions… that piercing of the veil into my soul. It feels exactly like that, a divine shiver. And we can all learn to enter into that divine place often if we only just learn to be still.

PART 4. MORE VISIONS

TODAY.

Oh Holy Spirit, possess me!

Possess my mind and my every thought!

Possess my tongue and my every word!

Possess my heart and my passions.

Possess my body, my hands and feet.

Possess the entirety of my life

And take me for Your glory.

Oh my Lord, my God

Praise Your Holy Name!

by Blue Tapp, 2020

Today, almost three years after the visions began, I still experience visions several times a week. God continues to teach me and draw me closer to Himself. I have done nothing to deserve this incredible gift. I am greatly humbled that God chose a sinner like me to forgive and bless in such an amazing way.

I personally benefit from these visions. They are rapturous experiences that also teach me so much. But they are not just for me alone. God began directing me from the very beginning, and continues to demand that I write everything down. I have faithfully recorded every vision, every locution, every word I believe God has told me over these three years, many journals worth of content so far.

I believe God wants certain others to hear the messages He is giving me. I have no idea how many people that might involve, maybe thousands, maybe only a handful. Even if it is only one person, that is enough. I must try my best to do the work that I believe God is calling me to do. And so I write and fill up these journals. And I pray, meditate and earnestly seek God every single day.

I don't use a timer anymore for my meditations. No need. They usually last about an hour and a half every morning now. My morning time with God has evolved to include not only meditation, but also regular communion, worship songs He has given me and memorized prayers. I will likely write another book delving more deeply into this service that I call 'Litos Ergos,' a public worship and communion service that celebrates and honors Jesus Christ.

In December 2019 I had a vision that Teresa came to me and put her hands on my head and prayed for me as she often does. Then I saw my own body lying face up on a long grey stone altar. The fiery glory of God descended from above and surrounded the altar. My body was completely engulfed by the flames. Energy pulsed throughout my entire body but no pain. God said, "You must be totally consumed by Me." This is my daily prayer now, that I will be totally consumed by God.

After Moses and the Israelites sacrificed animals to God 'the glory of the Lord appeared to all the people; fire came out from the presence of the LORD and consumed the burnt offering and the fat portions on the altar. And when all the people saw it, they shouted for joy and fell face down."[62] Could this be the same fiery "glory of the LORD" that I see in my visions?

Immediately after this, Aaron's sons, Nadab and Abihu, filled their censers and "offered unauthorized fire before the LORD, contrary to His command. So fire came out from the presence of the LORD and consumed them, and they died before the LORD."[63] Well that is disturbing. I must *always* be mindful of God's mighty holiness. I must never belittle the gravity of what God is showing me in these vision experiences. This is a terrifying gift, to be brought into the presence of the most holy God, even if only in a vision. Our ancestors in the Old Testament were terrified by their visions and angelic encounters. They usually fell flat on their faces in fear. I do not take this lightly.

God has pursued me, saved me, forgiven me, healed me, and blessed me. I owe Him my entire life. I owe Him every breath, every second of life I have left on this earth in this physical body. I commit myself to Him, all of me, my heart, mind, body, spirit and soul. I am not my own. I willingly choose to forfeit any decisions or control over my own life to God.

---

[62] *Leviticus 9:23-24 NIV*

[63] *Leviticus 10:1-2 NIV*

Lord Jesus, help me to accomplish this commitment. Give me wisdom, humility, and a heart that loves You above all else. Lord, help me to be obedient. I want to be consumed by You. Holy Spirit, possess me.

THE CRUCIFIXION

In December 2019. I had a vision in which Teresa introduced me to Mary, the mother of Jesus.

I was overwhelmed. I immediately knew who she was. I tried to pull my arm away from Teresa's grip as she tugged me toward Mary. I am not worthy to meet the mother of Jesus. Teresa pulled me forward. She grasped my shoulder and pushed me down to my knees in front of Mary.

I looked up into Mary's face and everything melted around me. Her beautiful cherubic smiling face captivated me. Her entire body shone brilliantly, her snow white skin and flowing robes were luminous. The powerful love and warmth emanating from her seemed almost tangible. It pressed into my soul. When she smiled at me, all of my fear instantly evaporated. I felt immediately safe in her comforting presence. She told me not to be afraid and placed her hands on top of my head. I could feel heat radiating out from her fingertips down through my body, a divine blessing. Her voice was melodic, like a singing bird.

She asked me to stand up and the three of us — Mary, Teresa, and I — stood together holding hands. Energy pulsed powerfully through our clasped hands. Everything around us changed, twisting around into a darkening whirlwind. I catapulted deeply into the meditation.

And then I stood on Golgotha in front of the cross. The sky above me was a raging tempest, black and purple and blood red. Lightning ripped across the sky. Thunder shook the ground. Icy wind bit into my skin. Shouting, pushing crowds of people in dirty tattered robes surrounded me.

I looked up and I saw Jesus hanging above me on the cross. His body was mangled, gashed horribly, exposed muscles quivering in pain. Rivers of blood dripped down His body onto the ground below. It was the most terrible sight I have ever seen.

He looked at me and said nothing, but His eyes pierced through my soul. He recognized me. Underneath the horrific wounded flesh I felt His stubborn embrace of impending death. He chose this. He chose to remain on that cross every agonizing second. Underneath the physical torment, He was completely God, completely aware, completely in control of His fate. He could have come down from that cross at any moment, instantly ending His horrific pain. He chose to stay there. His gaze conveyed all of this to me in an instant. He knew who I was. In the midst of being tortured, hung and murdered, He knew me. I was the reason He was even there.

I collapsed to the ground in shock. I pushed my face down to the ground. It was foul, clods of hard dirt covered with blood, guts, feces… gruesome. And I was lying in it. The foul earth was nothing compared to the horror of Christ's dying body hanging above me. I couldn't breathe. My mouth opened in a silent scream of terror.

Mary and Teresa pulled me to my feet, I was a sobbing rag doll. They held my right hand tightly and pushed it forward and up to touch the toes of Jesus. I pulled back but their hands were hard and firm. They pressed my shaking hand onto His foot. The instant my fingers touched his toes, a tremendous electricity blasted into me. His love instantly overwhelmed me and I willingly pushed my hand more firmly onto His foot. A hundred men couldn't pull me away from Him now. Mary and Teresa released me and stepped aside. As I gazed up at my beautiful dying Savior, my spirit screamed out His name over and over, "Jesus! Jesus! Jesus!"

His agony was appalling to behold. I could no longer bear it. I begged Teresa through my tears, "I don't want to see Him like this anymore. Please take me away from here."

The scene in front of me immediately transformed into the beautiful fiery glory of God that I have seen so often before. Its exquisiteness engulfed me and I rested. A voice whispered, "I will wipe all the tears from your eyes," and I felt a hand softly caressing my face.

Then everything disappeared and I was back in my physical room. As I wept and prayed I felt God instructing me, once again, to write *everything* down. This is my assignment, to write *all* of these visions down.

Several weeks later I again was transported to Christ's crucifixion in a vision. I stood in the crowd after Pontius Pilate had ordered to have Jesus beaten. I watched horrified with the others as the guards prepared to strike him with their whips. In the vision, God opened my eyes to see the spiritual realm during that momentous event. Angels surrounded Jesus. Hundreds of them filled the courtyard. Others hovered in the air above Jesus. They looked stunned, terror-stricken at what they were seeing. Many of them held their swords, ready to attack the guards, to end this horror.

God would not allow them to act. They could only watch helplessly as Jesus was flogged and beaten, waiting desperately for God to give them the signal to intervene. That signal never came. Jesus himself also held them back. He had given God His permission… "Not My will, but Yours be done." And so God was ripped in two so that we might be able to enter into union with Him.

On Golgotha, Jesus' broken body was surrounded by attending angels. They embraced Jesus' body as He was being nailed to the cross and stayed with Him as He hung there. They held tightly onto Him, caressing His wounds, kissing His body. They wept violently at His pain. They begged Him to say the word and let them take Him down from the cross… to let them destroy His murderers with their mighty swords. But Jesus would not allow them to do these things. They wept all the more as He refused their pleas. I was amazed at how deeply the angels love Jesus. They worship Him too. They were tortured by His pain.

The angels were forced to leave Him in the moments before He died. They wept bitterly, clinging desperately to His body as they were pulled away from Him by an invisible force.

Hoards of demons rushed in immediately when the angels left Him. Dark, hideous trolls of the underworld surrounded Jesus' body. They tortured His wrecked body as He hung there dying, slicing their talons into His skin and ripping His flesh further. They laughed and taunted as He gasped for His final breaths. They paraded their deformed bodies around the cross in triumph. I watched disgusted at their celebration after Jesus died. As His body was put into the tomb and the stone rolled into place, the demons erupted into a ghastly debaucherous party in front of the tomb. They maniacally laughed and mocked, toasting each other with gnarled claws raised in the air. Satan stood in their midst nodding at their obscene celebrations, his mouth twisting into a wicked smirk.

A faint light appeared on the horizon. It slowly grew stronger and brighter into a dazzling sun. The demons were too preoccupied in their disgusting orgy to notice. Then the stone blocking the cave entrance began to shake, almost imperceptibly at first and then faster and faster until it rolled backwards away from the mouth of the cave. Christ emerged alive from the tomb.

The demons abruptly stopped their revelries and turned to gape in horror at Jesus. Satan scowled, black eyes glowering in hatred at the figure standing in front of the empty tomb.

Christ was risen and glorious, alive, healed and whole. His body grew into an immense, brightly shining giant. He slowly raised His arm and pointed his finger accusingly as Satan and all his demons cowered beneath Christ's unflinching stare. They morosely slithered, banished into the now empty cave. And the stone was divinely rolled back into place by an invisible hand, trapping them all inside. Hallelujah.

THE PERPETUAL TRUTH OF JESUS

On the Christmas Eve service in 2019 at my mother's church I had a vision that the church was full of angels worshipping along with us. This has happened at every church service I've visited since my visions began. The angels seem so happy at church, dancing, singing, praising along with us. I've visited many different kinds of churches… charismatic, evangelical, protestant, catholic… and this has invariably been true. Regardless of whether the church seems fired up or dead, I always see angels worshipping with the attendees. We should find this so encouraging. Even though some churches may feel dead and useless to us, angels are still there. Whenever people gather together with even the most feeble intention to worship Jesus, beautiful things still happen in the spiritual realm.

At this particular service, my attending angel, who I often see, leaned down close to my face and smiled his huge smile, as he often does, and told me, "We get it. We understand what this [Christmas] means. Don't you see? This is why we worship Jesus."

Then I saw the nativity in my spirit. Mary and Joseph knelt in a dark stable on a chilly starry night. Mary held the baby Jesus in her arms. I watched from outside the stable looking through the open stable doors. Everything was dark and silent. The world slept through this pivotal event that profoundly changed the universe forever.

Then in the spirit I danced with my angel. He grabbed my hands and whirled me around and we laughed. It was so beautiful and filled with joy. How wonderful is the Christmas time of year when so many of us are celebrating the birth of Christ along with the angels.

In a later vision the glory of God changed into Jesus on the cross. Then the crucifixion changed into the nativity. And then back to the fiery glory of God. It kept shifting through these three things faster and faster until it just appeared to be the glory of God. I understood that God was showing me that all of these things — Jesus coming to earth, Jesus' crucifixion, and the glorified risen Savior — are simultaneously perpetually true. Eternity is not how we think of it... years, months, days, going on forever. In the spiritual realm there is no *time* so everything exists and is true all of the time. God is the ultimate truth of this reality.

This doesn't mean that Jesus is dying over and over again. Death only exists in this physical realm. Since God exists outside of time, Jesus' death on the cross, His life on earth, and the glorified Jesus can all be perpetually true. His blood shed on the cross continues to cover and cleanse us. The death of Jesus ripped apart the veil between the physical and spiritual realms. His resurrection defeated death for all eternity. This is a great mystery that I don't fully understand. That is okay. It is alright not to understand everything. Only God is omniscient. God understands all things and that is enough.

Jesus is perpetually watching and recognizing us as each one of us, in one way or another, comes to stand at the foot of the cross. We wrestle with the death of Christ and our own mortality in a million different ways. Or we don't. Some people instead choose to push the reality of God's death and our own mortality outside of their consciousness and so condemn themselves to a life of spiritual sleepwalking.

Just as Christ's death on the cross is perpetually true, He is also perpetually risen, perpetually glorified, and perpetually victorious over Satan (hallelujah). It is impossible for us with our finite, mortal brains to comprehend what it means to exist outside of time. God is not confined by the limitations of time as we are. It opens up infinite possibilities. This is how God can be omnipresent. This is how He is omniscient. This is how He can know each one of us personally and intimately.

Heaven is God's holy presence. God is here within us, all around us, in everything because God is omnipresent. The spirit world is all around us, right here, right now. This is what Jesus meant when He said, "The kingdom of heaven is at hand."[64] It is here now. We can't usually see it because there is a veil that shields us from it. Our physical flesh is the veil that separates us physical humans from the spiritual realm where God exists. The veil in the Jewish temple was torn when Christ died because His death and resurrection split the veil between the physical and spiritual realms. Now we *can* connect with and see into the spirit world sometimes because of Christ, who is our bridge between the spiritual and physical worlds. God *wants* to let us connect with the spiritual realm. God *wants* to let us in which is why Jesus came to earth as a human to begin with.

Sometimes God allows us to see into the other side. That's what I think happens when I have visions. There are things that sometimes make the veil thinner… music, nature… that is why we are deeply moved by such things.

---

[64] *Matthew 3:2 NKJV*

THE LOVE OF JESUS

In another intense vision in early in January 2020, I saw myself on my knees in a courtyard surrounded by onlookers. A Roman soldier held my bound hands out in front of me while another soldier stood behind me, prepared to strike me with a whip. I closed my eyes, cringing, waiting to feel the sting on my back. Instead as the whip hurled toward my body, Jesus suddenly appeared and stood between me and the whip with His arms outstretched. The whip's blows lacerated His back instead of mine over and over again.

Then I was again back in front of the cross on my face on the foul ground beneath Jesus. Jesus' blood dripped onto my kneeling body. The drops of blood should have been my blood. Jesus shed them for me instead.

Once again my surroundings transformed and I was back in the holy place. Jesus stood in front of me holding my hands in His… a parallel of the previous vision when the guard had held out my bound hands in front of me. Only now my outstretched hands were enclosed by the loving nail-scarred hands of Jesus. He softly repeated, "My child. My child. My child," as he held my hands and gazed into my eyes. So much love emanates from Jesus. His great love engulfs all of me, surrounds me and fills me. His love pours out over the entire earth, over every single human being who has ever lived. How much He loves us. We cannot comprehend such great love.

Jesus said, "Ask and it will be given to you; seek and you will find; knock and the door will be opened to you. For everyone who asks receives; the one who seeks finds; and to the one who knocks, the door will be opened."[65] This verse is actively happening to me. My daily meditations are me knocking on the door, seeking God, setting aside time for God to do whatever He wishes to do with me. These visions are me receiving from God and the door being opened. God is using these visions to open up my mind and teach me. When God imparts wisdom directly to my brain in a little explosion of knowledge, this is my Father in heaven giving good gifts to me.

He will give you good gifts too if you dive into Him with your whole soul. The riches of His love for us have no end. He is worthy of all of your love, your heart, mind, and soul. How God delights to give us good gifts such as these!

POWER OF PRAYER

Early in January 2020, I had a vision about the power of our prayers. The things I have seen in the holy place in my visions — all of the saints together holding hands praying for the world — this is happening in the spiritual realm when we, in the physical realm, pray. Prayer is so powerful.

---

[65] *Matthew 7:7-11 NIV*

Never doubt the power of prayer. The spiritual realm always responds to our prayers, whether we feel anything or not. Always.

Craig and I often visit other churches of our friends and family members. We used to call ourselves itinerant worshippers. It has been so fun, but has also been very spiritually beneficial. I am now able to see what happens in the spirit realm during these church services and it is exciting and encouraging. So far *every* church we've attended (Protestant, Catholic, Nondenominational, Charismatic, Non-Charismatic, etc.) has been filled with angels. When we sing praise songs and hymns, the angels sing with us. Sometimes the angels dance together like they are having a great party. They get excited and obviously love when the Bible is read.

I find this so reassuring. It might seem like nothing is happening in church sometimes. But something is always happening in the spiritual realm when we gather together at church, whether we feel it or not. Do not doubt that coming together to praise and worship God is so very *powerful.*

Another thing I have observed in my visions is that any time someone prays or focuses on God or worships, angels gather there. The more intense the prayer, the more people who gather together to worship, the more angels will be in attendance. We Christians should pray and gather more. Don't worry; there are plenty of angels to go around… the number of angels who exist is too great for us to even fathom, there are incomprehensively massive armies of them. Of course God's operation is going to be fantastically immense.

When the prophet Elisha's servant was afraid because they were surrounded by an enemy army, Elisha told him, "Don't be afraid… Those who are with us are more than those who are with them." And Elisha prayed, "Open his eyes, Lord, so that he may see." Then the LORD opened the servant's eyes, and he looked and saw the hills full of horses and chariots of fire all around Elisha."[66] I love this passage. I love that God allowed Elisha to see into the spiritual realm and that when Elisha asked, God opened his servant's eyes as well. How I pray for the Lord to open our eyes also to see His angels who are always around us. Just know that even if you can't see them, the angels are really there.

I have often observed in my visions that when we pray and worship, angels form an angelic whirlwind rotating upward from the earth up into the sky, like a gateway to the glory of God. Is this similar to Jacob's dream of a "stairway resting on the earth, with its top reaching to heaven, and the angels of God… ascending and descending on it?"[67] I see this angelic gateway often in my visions. Many times when the vision begins, I first see one towering angel with a sword standing out in front of me. He seems to be a sentry of some sort, tall and strong, wearing armor, very serious and powerful. His

---

[66] *2 Kings 6:16-17 NIV*

[67] *Genesis 28:12 NIV*

metal helmet covers his face so I do not see his expression, but he exudes strength and protection. I believe his role is a spiritual protector, not only of me but of the other angels too. After a short while he motions to the sky and other angels will appear swirling up above me in an angelic whirlwind twisting upward toward the heavens.

Sometimes the sky is filled with millions of angels swirling around above me. There are many different kinds of angels, different sizes and appearances. They are usually grouped together with others of the same appearance in layers. Each row is comprised of different kinds of angels. Each type of angel seems to have a unique identity and purpose. Some are small, young, cherubic and playful. Some are larger, very masculine and strong, carrying swords. Others play instruments or sing. One row consists of angels who appear feminine (most angels I have seen appear masculine) with beautiful flowing hair and long waving red dresses with tongues of holy fire emanating from them. What a glorious orchestra of celestial creatures this is, urging my soul heavenward!

The angels want so very much for us to understand how fantastically wonderful Jesus is. The angels love Him so much. I think they must often be exasperated by our blockheaded stupidity. But they understand how much Jesus loves us. They love us because of His love for us. Heavenly beings are capable of much deeper, greater love than we boorish humans can muster up while we exist in these physical bodies. How wonderful it will be when we have heavenly bodies of our own.

THE FUTURE.

I've got a new heart.

I've got a freed soul.

The story of the

Arrows is done.

First rays of morning,

Gold amber light.

Winter is over.

Spring has begun…

from "Morning"
song lyrics by Blue Tapp

A HEAVENLY WAR

In March 2020 I had a series of visions in which a heavenly battle took place. In the holy place I saw a great army of angels wearing armor and carrying swords. The angels rode horses and their heavenly cavalry galloped madly across the valley… millions of them going to war. They shook the entire valley. I could hear God's loud voice exclaiming, "My anger is hot! My anger is hot!" It was terrifying.

I fell to my stomach, mashed my face into the floor, and begged God to have mercy on us, please have mercy on us. God replied in a booming voice, "I will have mercy upon whom I will have mercy." That was not very comforting.

Then everything around me transformed. I floated above a great mass of people. Everyone gaped in terror at God's fiery holy glory hovering above them. Their bodies shook uncontrollably and they screamed, "I had no idea! I had no idea!"

This was identical to the very first vision I had many years before. Never in all the visions I have had since August 2019, had I ever seen that particular vision again until now. I have wondered since then if this is a vision of the end days that Jesus describes in Matthew:

> Immediately after the distress of those days 'the sun will be darkened, and the moon will not give its light; the stars will fall from the sky, and the heavenly bodies will be shaken.' Then will appear the sign of the Son of Man in heaven. And then all the peoples of the earth will mourn when they see the Son of Man coming on the clouds of heaven, with power and great glory. And He will send His angels with a loud trumpet call, and they will gather His elect from the four winds, from one end of the heavens to the other.
>
> Matthew 24:29-31 NIV

Many believe this is a prophecy of the second coming of Jesus Christ. Could this be what I saw in my very first vision almost two decades ago? How much I have learned since then. There are still so many mysteries.

Then God said to me, "No matter how much I show you during this life, you will still be shaking in fear and shouting out 'I had no idea!' when you first come face to face with Me. Everyone will... "

In a later vision, I felt great darkness and struggle. My entire physical body shook violently. I lay on my face and pounded the floor with my fists and feet. I cried out in tongues.

It was dark and I could see very little but continued to feel intense pain and turmoil. This lasted about ten minutes and then I felt myself being pulled backwards into a level further out from the battle. In this level I prayed hard for those now on the frontline where I had just been. I was still in darkness but could feel myself holding hands with saints all around me. We all prayed for the saints who were now on the frontlines. We were their support team. I stayed there for another ten minutes.

Then I was pulled even further out to another level to rest from the battle and regain strength. Out here I could finally see my surroundings. I held my arms out above my head in a "Y" and my legs spread out wide so that my body formed an "X." My hands and feet touched the hands and feet of saints all around me. We were all in the same "X" position, our hands and feet touching to create an immense human mesh all around the earth. Teresa was to my right. Dad and Grandma were there as well. I looked around and I could see all the saints around me… millions of men and women wearing different kinds of clothing from different time periods. I saw other nuns in habits. A man wore medieval armor. Some people were robed. Others were dressed in modern day clothing like me.

I understood that we each were to take turns on the frontline, and then move out to this outer ring to give prayer support to the others who were closer in. From this outer layer we could see the entire earth. We also could see all the people on the earth and we prayed for them as well. I saw that all of our souls are connected through time with God and the angels. I saw the concentric circles of angels spiraling out from the earth that I have seen before during my meditations. Only now I viewed these angelic whirlwinds from ten miles into space rather than my usual vantage point on the ground. We were all connected, people praying down below, our web of saints circling above, the angelic strings emanating heavenward from earth, the saints and angels fighting in darkness on the frontlines, and God's holy power. God's power flowed through all of us and into the souls on the earth. God uses us to conduct His power into the earth.

This is not some fun video game. This is a real war. And every single one of us are called to battle in this holy war against the forces of evil on earth. Prayer is warfare and this war takes place in our prayer closets. Pray, saints, pray.

*Finally, be strong in the Lord and in his mighty power.
Put on the full armor of God, so that you can take your
stand against the devil's schemes. For our struggle is
not against flesh and blood, but against the rulers,
against the authorities, against the powers of this dark
world and against the spiritual forces of evil in the
heavenly realms. Therefore put on the full armor of
God, so that when the day of evil comes, you may be
able to stand your ground, and after you have done
everything, to stand. Stand firm then, with the belt of
truth buckled around your waist, with the breastplate of
righteousness in place, and with your feet fitted with
the readiness that comes from the gospel of peace. In
addition to all this, take up the shield of faith, with
which you can extinguish all the flaming arrows of the
evil one. Take the helmet of salvation and the sword of
the Spirit, which is the word of God. And pray in the
Spirit on all occasions with all kinds of prayers and
requests. With this in mind, be alert and always keep
on praying for all the Lord's people.*

Ephesians 6:10-18 (NIV)

I have since gone to the frontlines in visions many times. In
another vision I stood together with other soldiers pushing the
enemy back. The battle raged. I was surrounded by a
cacophony of shouting and brutality. My body was pushed
violently about, but I felt no fear. I could feel God's strength
and courage flow through me as I held up my shield and
pushed forward with all my might in my vision. In the physical

realm, I yelled out in tongues and pounded the floor with my fists.

As I pushed forward in my vision, with my physical body convulsing and shouting out in tongues, suddenly a strange thought flashed into my mind... what if this is a trick of the enemy? What if I am speaking in a demonic tongue?

The same instant that thought sparked through my brain, in my vision I was pulled back off the frontline to a dark quiet place. Someone talked softly to me. In the darkness, I couldn't tell for certain who it was but I think it may have been Dad. His voice was quiet and reassuring. He gently explained that I can know for sure "from where my help comes" by asking these questions: What happens in my vision if I speak out the name of Jesus? How does the vision affect me? With anger or with praising God? With fear or peace? These tests help me discern and reassure me that these visions really are from God.

The voice continued to explain that all my experiences with demons in the past have prepared me for this. I have received extensive training in the warfare tactics of the enemy. I know how demons work, what they sound like, look like, how they make me feel. My encounters and battles with demonic forces have rendered me an experienced tactical spiritual soldier. I am certainly fallible of course and any strength I have is only from God. But God has perfectly, uniquely prepared me for this battle. All of my supernatural experiences that God has brought me through have taught me to recognize the strategies of the enemy.

I told God that I was ready to go back to the front line and I did go back for a little while before I was eventually pulled back out again. God sat me down in a beautiful field covered with soft velvet grass and told me to rest and build up my strength. I will need it. He told me, "You have been given weapons. Trust your training. Use your weapons. Have no fear."

April 4, 2020 was a national call to prayer and meditation at 9:45am. As I prayed, I again saw the mesh of saints encircling the earth. This time we were several layers thick. I kept seeing new people join in. I did go to the front lines but only for a very short time that day, perhaps because there were so many of us available to take turns. Never underestimate the power of our prayers. We need each others' prayers.

In another vision, I stood with hundreds or more other saints in a tremendous dimly lit cave. We all held hands in a big circle. In the center of the circle was an angel with a long sword fighting an enormous dragon. The angel was a muscle bound giant, a skillful sword wielding warrior. His agile strength mesmerized me as he blocked the dragon's vicious attacks with his sword.

The dragon was terrible, an immense serpentine fire spitting monster with razor teeth and claws.

It was a fierce battle. The angel repeatedly struck at the dragon with his sword but the dragon quickly twisted away from the sword strikes without injury. The dragon roared and fire exploded out from his mouth and nostrils. He swiveled his gargantuan head and shot out fire toward all of us as we scrambled backwards away from the flames. The angel appeared to be tiring, his movements grew sluggish. I feared he might lose this battle.

Then a line of saints with swords formed in front of us. Together they slowly moved forward step by deliberate step. The weary angel stepped aside as they encroached closer, surrounding and trapping the dragon within their circle, hemming him in tightly so that he could not twist his head around to attack. They plunged their weapons over and over into his writhing body, until finally he crashed to the ground. He was dead. We stood for a moment in silence, staring open-mouthed at his dead body. Then we erupted into cheers, exhausted from the battle but ecstatic at our victory.

I'm not sure what these visions mean. Are they showing what is happening in the spirit realm today? March 2020 was when the world was hit with the scourge of COVID-19. I am certain many battles indeed raged in the spirit realm at that time. Or am I seeing visions of something in the future? Perhaps God is preparing to send out a call to His bride, to call believers to Himself and reveal Himself to others in a great revival. Whenever Satan has become too powerful on earth, God either completely destroys (Tower of Babel, Sodom & Gomorrah, the flood) or He allows great calamities to cause his people to turn back to Him. I believe these visions of warfare are revealing that God is in the midst of a divine transformation of the earth or that it is coming, maybe soon.

After two months of warfare dreams, I had several visions of great celebration and peace. It appeared that the war was over. Millions of people and angels celebrated victory in the holy place. They were dancing, singing, laughing, smiling in a glorious celebration. People shouted, "Victory! The victory is done!" We praised God and sang with the angels "Holy Holy Holy Lord! God of power and might! Heaven and earth are filled with Your glory! Hosanna! Hosanna! In the highest!"

I fell on my face and begged God for this result, begged Him to draw Christians into their closets to pray. I took communion there and watched the elements turn into fire in my hands. As we held up our wine glasses, Jesus said, "The time is coming soon when you won't have to do this anymore. You will be with Me always." I heard a voice yelling "Drink." God said, "I pour out my blood over all the earth."

I saw Jesus holy and glorified on His throne. I knew that when this day comes, Jesus will no longer be perpetually on the cross. He will be alive and glorified forever. I saw the earth in the middle of our immense circle and it looked greener, bluer, cleaner than before. God said, "Behold I make all things new."

Hallelujah!

MY COMMISSION

This is my body
Eat and be filled
This is my blood
Drink of it and know me
This do in rememberance
This do in rememberance
This do in rememberance
Of me, of me

from "This Do in Rememberance"
song by Blue Tapp

I had an intense painful vision in March 2020. My physical body convulsed and I sucked air into my lungs with loud gasps. It felt like that first loud heaving inhale when my spirit returned back into my body after I died...deep, painful, gulping in air. God reminded me that spirits do not breathe air. They do not have beating hearts or flowing blood. The Holy Spirit replaces all of those things. Our time in the womb is a season encased in water... breathing water. Then we are born into this season and gasp in our first breath of air. We will remain here in this physical world gasping in breaths of air over and over and over again until we die and are born into our next season as spiritual realm beings. That will be quite an amazing upgrade.

How amazing, how glorious that God took on a human physical body gasping in air, with beating heart and flowing blood, to save us. How humbling. What an inconceivable sacrifice.

I've been taking communion alone every day during my meditations. It's been wonderful. Often Jesus comes to me in my vision to hand the wafer and cup to me in the spirit. Sometimes I am in the holy place while I take communion. All the other souls take communion with me in unison. So glorious. The wafer turns into a ball of fire in my palm. And the wine turns into a mixture of fire and water before I drink it.

Sometimes after taking communion we hold out our hands into the fiery glory of God in the center of our circle. When we pull our hands back out of the fire, small balls of fire remain in our palms. Sometimes we press the fire into our mouths or chests and feel the warmth of the glory of God coursing through our bodies.

During another meditation I found myself standing in a dark hallway. In the distance I heard music. I recognized that it was my song "This Do in Rememberance." It was being sung by a voice much more beautiful than mine, and was being played on some melodic instrument, perhaps a harp.

In my vision, I started walking through the darkness toward the music with hands out in front of me, blindly feeling my way down the walls of a maze of black hallways. Gradually I began to see a faint light far ahead of me. The music grew louder and the light grew brighter as I walked.

Eventually I came to a huge opening high up in the side of a sheer cliff. The floor and walls of the hallway ended abruptly in front of me. On all sides I could see jagged vertical rock where the walls and floor stopped. I stood at the end of the hallway, now a gaping precipice that opened out into the empty air thousands of feet up the rugged mountainside. Behind me was the cool darkness of the hallway. Far below me I could see the holy place in all its bright beauty, the lush green valley surrounded by steep snow topped mountains, the crystal waterfall and river.

The glory of the Lord swirled around me like a soft wind, gently lifted me up and carried me down toward the holy place. God's glory swirled around my arms and legs and moved my body into a graceful dance in the air. I laughed out loud at the fun of it. The wind softly lowered me into the valley and I was left standing in the velvety tall grass.

There were other people there. I saw my sweet little old dog, Satchie. She was young and happy with no grey hair, as I remembered her when she was a puppy. I saw my husband, Craig, his four grown children, Dad, Grandma, and my mom and brother. All the people I love came to greet me. Everyone looked young, beautiful, healthy, perfect. We hugged each other and laughed. It was so wonderful. Am I seeing the afterlife in these visions?

In another vision, I took communion and again the wafer and wine turned into fire before I consumed them. God said He has heard our prayers and is healing the world. He said He is protecting everyone who loves Him. I asked Him how I could help other people understand how wonderful He is. He told me to write, sing, and make art and it will happen. I was laying on my face and in the vision He anointed my feet with fire. He has anointed my tongue and hands before but this is the first time He has anointed my feet. This is my commission, to write all of these visions down and to use the gifts God has given me to point others to Jesus.

MY THOUGHTS ON WHAT ALL OF THIS MEANS

I believe that the crazy happenings in our world today are completely being orchestrated by God. It is a divine transformation when God is bringing us back to Himself as he did so many times with the Israelites in the Old Testament. Only this time God is calling the entire world.

I believe that God is ushering in a new time, a transformation, a great awakening, a fantastic spiritual revival when many more of us will recognize that God is on the throne. I'm not sure exactly how this is going to look. It could be accomplished through great catastrophes and hardships. If God so chooses, it could be a painless, peaceful transformation. I think it is likely to be events that are prophesied in Ezekiel, Daniel, Revelation, and by Jesus Himself. All I know for sure is that God is in charge of this, whatever it is. What an amazing time to be alive.

Here's where I believe my visions come into play... This transformation of the world is so big that God has called in reinforcements for His prayer warriors (the saints who have already died and are called to pray for us from where they now reside in the holy place). What God is doing in our world today is so big that He has called people who are still living in the physical world, people like me, and certainly multitudes of others, so that we can pray for the world along with all the saints. Wow.

At first, I thought this was all so fun and neat that I got to have these amazing visions and pray for the world... I had no idea of the gravity of what I was being called to participate in. I was like a little kid thinking it was all a fun game. But this is no game. I am so honored, so infinitely blessed, to be among the people called to participate in this.

You are also being called, as is everyone on this earth. This entire physical time period we currently live within is God calling each one of us to Himself. Please know that you are part of this great cosmic story that has been happening from the beginning of time. If you struggle with depression, please know that the God who created the universe knows you intimately and wants to heal you and give you a victorious life. Please search within your soul in stillness and find this wonderful Savior who loves you. Please join me. Please join with the saints in this glorious adventure.

So I invite you, reader, to pray along with me and with all of God's saints. Pray for the world. Pray that people will become spiritually awakened and seek God. Pray that God will open people's eyes to understand His sovereignty. Pray that people will learn and believe in Jesus' great love and sacrifice for us. Pray for victory over Satan and his demons. Pray for God's kingdom come, His will be done. Lord, hear our prayer. Glory to God's holy Name forever!

CONCLUSION.

Craig and I have now been called to practice our faith in the countryside. After Craig retired in 2021, we purchased a farm near Branson, Missouri, where we are learning to homestead. We have named our farm Hermit's Way Homestead. It is a place where we and others will be able to escape from the busy loudness of the world in order to be still with God. God has given us a vision of building a "Healing Farm" where we will feed people both spiritually and physically.

(Learn more about our homestead at https://www.hermitsway.com/ and watch some really funny videos of our homestead adventures at https://www.youtube.com/c/HermitsWayHomestead)

My visions have continued to happen to me usually several times per week. The wild vision adventures continue. I don't know why God has chosen to grant such amazing gifts to little ol' stupid me. In the Bible, God often chooses the worst of the worst humans in which to work the miraculous. So you've read my story and you know that I most definitely would qualify as the worst of the worst.

Sometimes I have this little nagging feeling that having these wonderful visions is too good to be true. I'm afraid to trust it. Could I be making all of this up afterall? I don't think I am. I think I know the difference between my imagination and reality. But do I really? Is it possible to think that something that originates in your imagination is real? Of course it is. I could just be crazy after all. So I do worry about this sometimes. Usually after a time of doubt, I will have a vision experience so intense that I *know* it is real. Some of my visions are so potent that I know positively I am not making this up. My imagination is pretty active but it's not *that* powerful. I'm not creative enough to come up with all of these crazy things myself.

Still I doubt sometimes. I think having that little nagging doubt is actually good. Hopefully it will keep me humble. If that nagging feeling ever goes away, then I should probably worry. We should always test everything. No one should ever assume that every little thing that comes through during our meditations is really from God. I assume my imagination may contribute a little bit sometimes without me realizing it. I assume my interpretations of what I see could often be incorrect as well. Thinking that everything that flies through your brain is unquestionably from God is a huge prideful mistake. To be human is to be imperfect. The physical human brain will never be capable of completely understanding all truth. I could be wrong about everything. I am fallible. Everyone is. I make mistakes all the time. Everyone makes mistakes. We must always question and try to test any visions or messages or prophecies or any supernatural thing against Scripture and consulting Biblically grounded believers. We can always be wrong.

I do believe all of this. Really I do. And I've either become completely insane or there really *is* something to this. If I *am* insane then I can tell you it's the loveliest crazy in the universe.

I didn't want to write this book. I know that many people will never believe the stories I tell in these pages. There is nothing I can do to convince the doubters and really I have no intention of trying.

My only goal is to be obedient to what I believe God has instructed me to do. And what God keeps telling me to do is to write all of this down. I assume that means somebody, somewhere will eventually read this. I'm not necessarily happy about that. Obeying God in this doesn't mean people won't think I'm crazy. They most certainly will. That doesn't mean people won't think I'm making all this up for attention. Some people will definitely think that. It doesn't mean it will be anything big or that I will even ever know anything about it. But it will be being obedient to God's will. And God can do whatever He wants with that. And so I write.

And so I've written this book. And it is my fervent prayer that something in this book will bless you and draw you closer to God as well. And if you struggle with depression as I did, I pray that my story will help you also find healing. Thank you for reading my story. May God bless you and keep you.

Searching for My Savior

I stumble over jagged rocks in search of
An obscure path of righteousness,
But His word beckons from His promises
And washes through the obscurity,
Giving sight to my sin-blinded eyes,
Searing through the toughened scars of an old sinful man —
A defiant, stupid, ignorant old man.

Put him on the tree and pound in the nails,
That old man who oppresses my feeble endeavors.
Crucify him who defies the one who was crucified.
Dismember him limb by limb, bone by bone, piece by piece,
And replace each part with a part of my Lord.

Pluck out the eye that finds faults and errors;
And give one that sees the perfection of Jesus.
Cut out the tongue that speaks lies and gossip;
And give one that sings praise to my Lord.
Break off the hand that greedily clutches the world;
And give one that works to serve my Savior.
Tear out the heart that is proud and selfish;
And give one that loves with the love of Christ.
Kill the mind that lusts and despises:
And give one that seeks first the King of all Kings.

by Blue Tapp, 1989

~ ~ ~ end ~ ~ ~

216

DID YOU ENJOY THIS BOOK?

Please leave a review!

Use the QR code below to go directly to the review form:

ABOUT THE AUTHOR

Blue Tapp is a writer, artist, photographer, musician, and homesteader. She has an A.A. in Fine Arts, B.A. in English, M.A. in English Literature, and completed Ph.D. coursework in Rhetoric & Composition. She has run her own website development company, Blue's ArtHouse Graphics & Web Design, since 1997.

Blue writes inspirational nonfiction and speaks about seeking God through meditative prayer, healing from depression, and deliverance from demonic oppression. She is available for speaking engagements and podcast interviews. Email inquiries to bluetapp@gmail.com.

Blue and her husband, Craig Scheffer, live and homestead in Blue Eye, Missouri, where they raise chickens, ducks, rabbits, and sheep and grow their own food. Follow their homesteading adventures at hermitsway.com.

Contact / Follow Blue

bluetapp.com • facebook/blue.tapp
twitter.com/BlueTapp • instagram.com/bluetapp/
truthsocial.com/@BlueTapp • rumble.com/c/c-1204664
youtube.com/channel/UCo36NW3KqOuUDpl2g362AuA